M000164191

Heroines:

THE BOLD, THE BAD AND THE BEAUTIFUL

JESSICA RUSTON

LONG BARN BOOKS

Published by
LONG BARN BOOKS
Ebrington, Gloucestershire GL55 6NW

Set in Sabon
Printed and Bound by Compass Press Ltd
ISBN 10: 1-902421-15-9
ISBN 13: 987-1-902421-15-5

FOR THE HEROINES – EACH AND EVERY ONE

Contents

Introduction

⁓

DID YOU MEAN TO SEARCH FOR 'HEROES?' Came the helpful suggestion when I typed 'Heroines' into an internet search engine.

I looked up Heloise, the medieval scholar whose passionate correspondence with her former lover Abelard has made the pair a by-word for romance. SEE ABELARD says *Chambers Biographical Dictionary*.

What's wrong with heroes? Nothing at all. It's just time to put the girls first, and celebrate the wealth of women who have been Bold, Bad and Beautiful – and sometimes all three.

When I started to ask people who their heroines were, some names cropped up again and again – Florence Nightingale, Odette Hallowes, fine examples of women of virtue and courage – but it quickly became clear that heroines were coming from a wide variety of different and sometimes surprising quarters. The word means different things to different people. Some women were admired simply for their wit, their passion, their amazing names or their taste in shoes.

Some women just stand out from the crowd and refuse to be ignored. They inspire, they challenge and they provoke.

It quickly became clear that people were excited by the idea of Heroines, and spoke readily and enthusiastically about women they admired and who had inspired them. Heroines are clearly as important today as they ever were and they are not just dusty relics from history textbooks – plenty of those included here are alive now.

One woman, who was mentioned frequently and by a wide variety of people, was Dame Judi Dench. As an actress she is beyond compare. She has played almost all of the major female Shakespearean roles, indeed, many of the major female roles by any playwright. She has been Ophelia, Juliet, Iris Murdoch and Queen Victoria, and 'M'. She is the epitome of professionalism, a hard-working actress who has never allowed her fame to get in the way of her job, shooting scenes for the latest *Bond* film at the same time as playing the lead in a West End play, complete with two matinees a week. She has a wonderful sense of humour, and practical jokes. But as noted by Philip Bretherton in John Miller's biography of her, she is always the first to give the joke away, because she is always the first to laugh. When hiding from the director during rehearsal one day, Judi crawled into a piece of furniture, but "the metal cabinet she was in started to shake, and that's what gave it away". She has the sort of beauty that is admired by both men and women, with famously twinkling eyes and cheekbones to die for. But above all, she is kind, possessing a warmth and generosity of spirit that is apparent both in person and in performance. I am honoured that she has agreed to write this foreword.

Foreword

BY DAME JUDI DENCH

~

Few people come under the title of heroines, to my mind. How would I define a heroine? As somebody who inspires you to do better things? Reach for higher things? Not to emulate, but set your sights higher. They certainly don't need to be perfect – who's perfect anyway? My father's hero was Napoleon.

Peggy Ashcroft has been a major heroine in my life, since the early 1950s, when I saw her play Imogen, in *Cymbeline*, and Cleopatra, both at Stratford-upon-Avon, and those performances are still absolutely clearly etched in my mind. There was something profoundly touching about them.

Later, I performed with her in *The Cherry Orchard*, as Anya to her Ranevsky. She was wonderful, and when I played the same character years later, I could still hear the cadences of her voice in the role.

She was funny, naughty, inspirational, and she became a really wonderful friend, advising me – once telling me, "Whatever you do, don't play Lady Bracknell" – (advice which I did not take), and supporting me. She led quite a tortured life – but a passionate life. That's what it is for me I think – passion. She definitely had an effect on me personally. Very, very, funny. And rude.

Sadly I did not get to say goodbye to her. When I went to visit her in the Royal Free Hospital the registrar took me aside and told me she had died not long before. I will never forget her Queen Margaret in the Wars of the Roses cycle, at Stratford. She is still so much in my mind. How lucky, to have worked with one's heroine.

Some people stamp a brand on you. It's not to do with achievement; it's to do with the individual, their persona. Somebody who you kind of understand, and who is inspirational. And Peg was that.

Judi Dench

Not so Dumb Blondes

JORDAN/KATIE PRICE

*"Like God for Voltaire,
if Jordan did not exist, it
would be necessary to
invent her"*
Belle du Jour.

Her *autobiography* Being Jordan
has sold more than a million
copies, and describing a book-signing
attended by nearly 1,000 women,
Carole Cadwalladr of The
Observer remarked that "I
haven't seen such a display of
female devotion since Diana's funeral".
Outspoken, honest and a shrewd business-
woman, Katie Price has built her alter-ego Jordan into one
of the most familiar faces in Britain today. Named 'Cover
Girl of the Decade' by Loaded magazine, she has been on
thousands of front covers, including that of Playboy.

Jordan is an easy target for abuse and condescension, with her improbably over-enhanced breasts, hair and tan, but the false trappings conceal one of today's non-synthetic celebrities. She is unashamedly girly, marrying her pop star groom in a candy pink frock so over the top in its spangliness that it made the costumes from *Strictly Come Dancing* look restrained. She knows what she wants, she knows how to get it, and she won't let anything or anyone stand in her way.

BARBIE has had more than 80 careers, starting as a teenage fashion model; she has been a palaeontologist, rock star, a medic Sergeant, and has run for President not once but twice. Her campaign focused on educational opportunities for girls and on animal rights. Her pets have included 21 dogs, 14 horses, 3 ponies, 6 cats, a parrot, a chimpanzee, a panda, a lion cub, a giraffe and a zebra. Unfortunately she was not elected as President on either occasion, but continues to expand her CV, with sojourns in all areas of the military, as an astronaut, and a rock star. Barbie Millicent Rogers has five sisters, and has, sadly, recently split from her long-term beau, Ken.

TWIGGY The iconic '60s model, famous for her elfin looks, was the first celebrity to 'become' a Barbie doll. Pencil thin, with huge eyes, emphasised by spidery false eyelashes, she was the original supermodel, and the face of her era, despite working as a model for only 4 years. The first model, if not celebrity, to merchandise herself, Twiggy clothing, pencil cases, lunchboxes and a board game made her a brand name. She was also the first model to be immortalized in *Madame Tussaud's*.

DOLLY PARTON How fabulous to have your own theme park, named after you (*Dollywood*, in Tennessee's Smoky Mountains). She's probably the most successful female Country artist ever, with a collection of awards as large as her enormous hair and cartoon breasts. Her theme park and other attractions have brought huge economic development to a previously extremely poor and struggling region. She was also the first person to be awarded the Good Housekeeping *Seal of Approval.*

"I'm not offended by all the dumb blonde jokes because I know I'm not dumb – and I'm also not a blonde."

JEAN HARLOW, the Platinum Blonde, was rubbished as an actress, but set such a trend with the shade of her hair that Howard Hughes offered a $10,000 reward to any hairdresser able to recreate its exact shade. One of the original blonde bombshells, she was linked to various mobsters including Bugsy Siegel, and was Marilyn Monroe's idol; Marilyn is said to have kept a scrapbook of pictures of her.

VERONICA LAKE was arguably most famous for her curtain of blond hair rippling over one eye, and when, during the war, she changed to a more practical style, her popularity plummeted.

~

Hitchcock Blondes

Ingrid Bergman
Grace Kelly
Kim Novak
Eva Marie Saint
Janet Leigh
Tippi Hedren
Carole Lombard

~

BRIGITTE BARDOT turned her back on her career as an actress and her status as the original sex kitten in the 1970s, in order to dedicate herself to being an animal rights activist, and making other forms of political protest. The epitome of doe-eyed, long-limbed sensuality, she transformed her life and sold off her jewellery collection to raise money for her work, and despite angering many with some controversial remarks, she is one of the world's most influential animal activists.

DEBBIE HARRY, rock-chick bottle blonde and lead singer of *Blondie*, became the oldest female singer in the UK to have a number one hit in 1999, at 54. Full of attitude and spike heels and fun.

~

JOANNA TROLLOPE'S HEROINES

Mary Kingsley (the Victorian traveller)
Tina Turner
P.D. James
Princess Alexandra
Lisa Jardine
Florence Nightingale (not forgetting pre- Scutari...)

~

DUSTY SPRINGFIELD had an unforgettable voice. Haunting and husky and full of heart. She also had the sort of lacquered beehive that defied gravity.

GRACE KELLY had two rather different phases of life and fame, first as an actress, star of Hitchcock films and Westerns, and then as Princess Grace, wife of Albert II of Monaco. Coolly beautiful and elegant, her looks were at their serene best when she married – Albert commissioned Fleurissimo, by Creed, for their wedding; it was designed to contain all the flowers in her bouquet. After her marriage she retired from acting.

~

Blonde Heroines of Fiction

Goldilocks
Cinderella
Alice in Wonderland
Miss Piggy
Elle Woods (Legally Blonde)
Tinkerbell
Lorelei Lee (Gentlemen Prefer Blondes)

~

BARBARA WINDSOR, *Carry On* Queen of the double-entendre and now landlady of *Eastenders'* Queen Vic, her raucous giggle is dirty and warm and infectious.

PAULA YATES was a sharp, smart, sexy peroxide blonde who flirted the pants off nearly everyone who met her. Early host of the influential music show *The Tube*, along with Jools Holland. Later, with her husband Bob Geldof, she was the driving force behind the hugely successful *The Big Breakfast*, where she interviewed celebrities on a vast double bed. Those who knew her speak of her warmth – she seemed to gather people in to her brightly coloured world, and had that talent for making people feel as if they were the only focus of her attention. Fiercely intelligent and passionate, she wrote on everything from blondes to childcare, and her photography book *Rock Stars in Their Underpants* was called "the greatest work of art in the last decade" by Andy Warhol.

"At a time when television's version of womanhood was either brainy and plain, or pretty and dumb, Paula Yates broke the mould, by being precisely what she wanted to be. She was frighteningly clever, outstandingly witty, intuitive and original; she was a free-thinker, and her shoes matched her handbag."
Muriel Gray, journalist and arts commentator, and former co-host on *The Tube*.

MARILYN MONROE. More conspiracy theories and rumours surround her life and death than those of almost any other woman, save Princess Diana. Marilyn's image is instantly recognisable, the world over, and her name and references to her continue to appear in songs, films, art, cartoons, you name it, and her poses are imitated in advertising, theatre, photography and fashion...A captivating mixture of innocence and sex, curiosity and sensuality, Marilyn was the Ultimate Blonde.

Marilyn Miscellania

Hugh Hefner, owner of Playboy *magazine, bought the crypt adjoining Marilyn's for $85,000.*
She was the magazine's first cover girl in 1953.
She was voted Sexiest woman of the Century by People magazine in 1999.
When she sang her famous version of Happy Birthday to John F Kennedy, she had to be sewn into her dress, which was later sold for $1.26 million at Christie's.
There are almost 700 biographies of Marilyn in the English language alone.

"I don't want to make money. I just want to be wonderful."

Leaders of Men

~

MARGARET THATCHER

"To wear your heart on your sleeve isn't a very good plan. You should wear it inside, where it functions best."

The longest serving Prime Minister since Gladstone, and the first ever female one, Margaret Thatcher divides opinion, but few would deny that she is one of the most influential politicians ever. She always acted with conviction, and in doing so, changed the face of Britain for ever.

~

PENNY VINCENZI'S HEROINES

Scarlett O'Hara and Margaret Thatcher

Mrs T didn't have a 16" waist, nor was she the belle of 3 counties, though she did have the Presidents of 3 countries – France, Russia and America – in the palm of her hand. Otherwise, she and Scarlett were virtually identical – strong willed, incredibly brave, refusing to admit defeat ever, ground-breaking in their own way, an example of their own sex while both fairly dismissive of it. One can imagine as easily Scarlett beating down the unions as Mrs Thatcher shooting a rapacious Yankee dead and dressing up in the drawing room curtains rather than admit poverty, and both of them adopting 'Tomorrow is another day' as their battle-cry.

~

Head of state of 16 countries, QUEEN ELIZABETH II has reigned for 53 years, and has now celebrated her 80th birthday, when the Poet Laureate wrote that her greatest attribute was constancy. Graceful, dignified and wise, with a mischievous sense of humour, she is said to have responded to a shopkeeper who saw her and commented that she looked very much like the Queen, "How very reassuring!"

EVA PERON became famous in Argentina initially as an actress, playing historical heroines in radio dramas, and was known as 'Senorita Radio'. She met Colonel Juan Peron, her future husband, when he asked for her help with an earthquake appeal. Shortly after their marriage her new husband was arrested, and Eva has been popularly credited with organising the protests that led to his release. She was an influential campaigner for Peron during his presidential bid, and became the first woman in Argentine history to appear in public campaigning alongside her husband (quite a trendsetter, Evita – apparently she was also the first woman in public life in the country to wear trousers...). She made many charismatic and influential speeches in support of Juan Peron, and later, of herself, as she fought to win the Vice-Presidency, a political move that was violently opposed by the army. Her death, aged just 33, sent Argentina into national mourning – businesses closed and people stopped in the streets when it was announced on the radio. A million spectators attended her lying-in-state, and when her coffin was processed through the streets before her official burial seventeen people were crushed to death in the mêlée.

But Evita's story does not end with her death. Plans for her body to be entombed in the base of an enormous statue were halted when Juan Peron was overthrown; a military dictatorship took over the country, and hid her body, worried that it would inspire revolution. During Juan Peron's exile all sorts of wild claims were made about what had happened to her body, until in 1971 it was revealed that it had been

stored under a false name, in a Milanese crypt. It was eventually returned to Buenos Aires, where it now resides in a secure tomb said to be strong enough to withstand nuclear attack.

BRUNHILDE – Queen of the Franks, Visigoth princess and Queen of Austrasia, Brunhilde inhabited a time and place far removed from anything we can imagine now. She lived from approximately 545-613 and ruled over parts of Austrasia – which is present day Eastern France, Western Germany, Belgium and the Netherlands.

Opinion has always been divided over Brunhilde. She has been presented as a great stateswoman, a model queen – and as a tyrant. The death of her sister Galswintha, at the hands of her husband and his mistress, prompted Brunhilde to convince her husband Sigebert to wage war against the Western Franks. This passionate hatred for her brother-in-law characterised the rest of Brunhilde's life, and she struggled against him until she was betrayed by the Frankish nobles. There are various versions of her death, but according to the *Liber Historiae Francorum*:

Then the army of the Franks and Burgundians joined into one, all shouted together that death would be most fitting for the very wicked Brunhilda. Then King Clotaire ordered that she be lifted on to a camel and led through the entire army. Then she was tied to the feet of wild horses and torn apart limb from limb. Finally she died. Her final grave was the fire. Her bones were burnt.

CATHERINE THE GREAT or Princess Sophia Augusta Frederika of Anhalt-Zerbst, to give her her birth name, did not, as legend has it, die having sex with a horse, but, more prosaically, of a stroke. She was promised to Grand Duke Peter Fedorovich at the age of 16, in the customary arranged marriage. Peter was apparently a weak man, physically and emotionally, and was childish and hated Russia, of which he was due to become ruler. Their engagement was not a happy one. Peter contracted both measles and smallpox, which left him scarred, bald, and bitter. He began to drink heavily. By the time they married, Peter was unable to consummate their union, and Catherine was desperately unhappy, writing soon after the ceremony "I should have loved my new husband, if only he had been willing or able to be in the least lovable". She focused on intellectual pursuits, and eventually had a son (after Peter underwent an operation which restored normal sexual functions). But Peter's mother, the Empress, removed the child to her own quarters, where he remained for months and Catherine was forbidden to see him.

When the Empress died and Peter became the new Tsar, Catherine's situation became more miserable and dangerous still. Peter flaunted his mistress, and Catherine suspected he intended to dispose of her in favour of the woman. With the help of members of the Imperial Guard Catherine deposed her husband and became Empress.

She began a campaign to improve Russia's fortunes, concentrating on areas such as agriculture, mining and the fur trade, and industry boomed. She then turned her attention to education, founding a girl's boarding school, and ensuring that villages had adequate schooling facilities. She then tackled the smallpox epidemic, bringing a Scottish expert to the country to inoculate her, as an example to others, and once this had been declared a success, established vaccination centres in Moscow and St Petersburg. She founded the country's first College of Medicine, and decreed there must be a hospital for each provincial capital. In the arts, she commissioned the building of the Hermitage and the Royal Palaces.

Baron de Breteuil wrote of her:

"This princess seems to combine every kind of ambition in her person. Everything that may add lustre to her reign will have some attraction for her. Science and the arts will be encouraged to flourish in the empire, projects useful for the domestic economy will be undertaken. She will endeavour to reform the administration of justice and to invigorate the laws; but her policies will be based on Machiavellianism; and I should not be surprised if in this field she rivals the king of Prussia...This passionate princess, still held in check by the fear and consciousness of internal troubles, will know no restraint once she believes herself firmly established."

Catherine said "I shall be an autocrat, that's my trade; and the good Lord will forgive me, that's his."

MOTHER JONES became an American labour leader after the deaths of her husband and four children in a yellow fever epidemic, in 1867, and the subsequent loss of all her possessions in the great fire of Chicago in 1871. Lesser women might have crumpled in the face of such loss, but not Mother Jones. She became a fearless campaigner for the rights of miners and child workers, travelling continuously, encouraging – if not downright bullying – people to stand up for their rights, saying "I'm not a humanitarian; I'm a hell-raiser." She brought women, children and African-Americans into her strikes, and staged pageants where a child was crowned Queen of the Strikers. Dubbed the "grandmother of all agitators" by the US Senate, she was buried near the graves of strike victims in the coalfields of Illinois.

~

BEL MOONEY'S HEROINES

– all for reasons of strength:
Boadicea
Elizabeth I
George Eliot
Emmeline, Christabel and Sylvia Pankhurst
Rebecca West
Simone de Beauvoir
Wonderwoman
Greenham Common Women
Germaine Greer
Aung San Su Kyi
…and of course there are many more.

~

ELIZABETH I

Daughter of Anne Boleyn and Henry VIII, Elizabeth was brought up by governesses after her mother's execution in 1536, when Elizabeth was not yet 3 years old. Her step-mother, Katharine Parr, took an interest in her, ensuring she

received a broad education, including tuition in the art of public speaking, ordinarily unheard of for women. She was crowned in 1558, to great fanfare, and immediately set about establishing a religious structure for the country. Her reluctance to marry caused political unease amongst her ministers, as marriage was a way of forming and maintaining alliances with other countries. But she would not be bullied, saying that she would prefer to be a 'beggar woman and single, far rather than queen and married.'

Her reign is often referred to as the Golden Age. Her court was a centre of learning, England rose as a powerful force in

Europe and prospered economically. Francis Drake circumnavigated the globe, England colonised North America, and Shakespeare, Marlowe and Ben Jonson wrote some of the greatest works of literature ever during her reign. One of the most popular monarchs ever, her troops fought off the Spanish Armada, and Elizabeth made a famous speech promising to live or die with them if necessary, and saying "I know I have the body of a weak and feeble woman, but I have the heart and stomach of a King, and a King of England too."

CONDOLEEZZA RICE is exhaustingly well qualified and accomplished. Speaker of 5 languages, holder of a PhD, as well as a handful of honorary degrees, she is the first African-American woman (and only the second

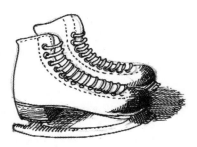

of her race, and gender) to hold the title of Secretary of State. At the time of writing she is fourth in line to succeed the President, a higher placing than any woman previously. She's also a concert pianist and competitive ice skater. According to the official website since January 2005, in her capacity as secretary of state she has travelled 451, 662 miles, notching up 228 hours 56.4 minutes of flight time.

EMPRESS DOWAGER WU ZETIAN *was the only female to rule China as monarch, in 690.*

Spies and Secret Agents

~

"They are all our mothers and sisters, you would not be able to either learn or play in freedom today, yes, you may not even have been born, if such women had not stood their soft, slender bodies before you and your future like protective steel shields throughout the Fascist terrors."
Odette Hallowes, 1993, speaking at Ravensbrück.

ODETTE HALLOWES'S career as a secret agent came about by accident, when she applied to the wrong department of the War Office. She worked as a courier in the South of France until 1943, and her betrayal by a Frenchman in whom she had placed her trust. Like many others she kept her silence through years of torture at the hands of the Gestapo – unlike many others, she survived to tell the tale, and died in 1995.

STELLA RIMINGTON

"I've never been one to retreat at the first whiff of gunshot"

The first woman Director-General of MI5, Stella Rimington caused an uproar in 2001 when she published *Open Secret,* about working for the Secret Service – although the book is actually less of an exposé of clandestine operations than a memoir of her life as 'Housewife Superspy'. A staunch upholder of women's rights throughout her career, she blazed something of a trail for women in the secret service.

Her agents were often initially extremely unhappy about working with a woman. When she was pregnant and sent to France to interview a potential informer, her condition was seen as so acutely embarrassing for all concerned that she was made to interview the man from behind a screen.

In 1991 she was appointed Director-General, the first to hold the position whose name was made public, with which announcement came a huge amount of unwanted exposure for her and her family, eventually resulting in her having to move house because of the press attention, complaints from her neighbours and security issues. All this was going on while she and her daughters were still expected to go about their everyday lives under assumed identities – though quite how this was meant to work is unclear.

On retirement from MI5 she took up the role of Non-Executive Director, before embarking on writing and publishing her autobiography because she 'has always wanted to bring some daylight into the world of intelligence', a decision that caused ructions throughout the security service, and one which came in for much criticism, and lost Rimington friends and allies.

~

Not all of them were spies, but the BOND GIRLS *have glamour, fabulous bikinis, and even better names.*

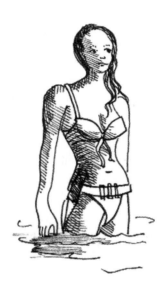

Honey Ryder
Pussy Galore
Domino Derval
Fiona Volpe
Tracy Vincenzo
Mary Goodnight
Anya Amasova
Octopussy
Pam Bouvier
Natalya Simonova
Jinx
Tatiana Romanova
Kissy Suzuki
Tiffany Case
Plenty O'Toole
Solitaire
Holly Goodhead
May Day
Christmas Jones
Molly Warmflash
And, of course, Miss
Moneypenny...

MATA HARI (Margaretha Geertruida Zelle MacLeod)

At 19 Margaretha, a milliner's daughter from the Netherlands, married Captain Rudolf Macleod, a man twice her age, after answering a personal advertisement of his for a wife. He was a Dutch colonial army officer, and they moved to Java, where she learned some of the sensuous dances for which she became known later. They had two children together, despite the fact that her husband was an alcoholic philanderer. The marriage eventually crumbled after their son was poisoned by the servants, allegedly in revenge against McCloud's rape of one of the servant's daughters.

Having left her husband and with a young daughter to support, Margaretha worked as a circus horse rider, and an artist's model, and also slipped into various informal 'arrangements' with wealthy men. One of these was a Baron who gave her the idea of becoming an exotic dancer, and helped her develop the character of Mata Hari, an Indian princess whose seductive dance of the veils had been passed down from her ancestors. She was an immediate sensation.

Despite her success as a dancer, she continued to conduct discreet liaisons for money with an assortment of influential men from various walks of life.

Suspicion fell upon her with the outbreak of World War I because of her acceptance of gifts and money from these very clients – were these donations for sexual services rendered, or a more sinister form of assistance? Her messages were intercepted and it was her alleged use of a German code number which convinced the authorities that she was a spy. She went to trial in 1917, proclaiming during the course of her hearing "Harlot, yes. But traitor? Never!" Sadly this failed to convince the court, however, and she was found guilty of spying and so causing the deaths of thousands of soldiers.

She went before the firing squad on October 15, 1917. Legend has it that she did so wearing a fur coat with nothing underneath, and when her executioners raised their guns to fire, she blew them a kiss and whipped up her coat.

EMMA PEEL, of *The Avengers*, wore a leather catsuit, drove a Lotus Elan at breakneck speed, was a mistress of martial arts, a certified genius, and an expert fencer. What's not to love?

HARRIET TUBMAN A former slave, Tubman was an important member of the Underground Railroad, helping hundreds of slaves escape during the later part of the 19th century. She used a variety of disguises to evade slave-catchers, proudly stating that she 'never lost a passenger'.

She served as a spy for the North during the Civil War, and, in the first American military campaign planned and carried out by a woman, she led a raid in South Carolina which allowed many more slaves to escape.

LADY PENELOPE CREIGHTON-WARD, or Lady P, the British Agent for International Rescue, operates from her English country mansion and her pink, amphibious Rolls Royce, FAB1.

JOSEPHINE BAKER performed at the Folies Bergères in a tiny skirt made of bananas, holding Chiquita, her pet leopard, on a diamond leash, who added to the drama of her show by frequently

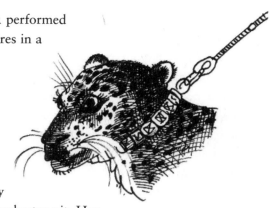

escaping into the orchestra pit. Her success and popularity made her work for the French Resistance – for which she was later awarded the Croix de Guerre – easier to accomplish. She would smuggle secret messages on her music sheets, and worked as a Red Cross nurse. She was also a civil rights campaigner, refusing to perform in segregated theatres, and speaking at the 1963 March on Washington, where she looked out over the crowd and said "Salt and pepper. Just what it should be."

She was married numerous times (not all of them officially – once the ceremony took place in an otherwise empty church in Mexico), and adopted 12 children from around the world, that she called her 'rainbow tribe'.

On her death in 1975, 20,000 people crowded the streets of Paris to see her funeral procession, and she became the first American woman to be buried in France with military honours.

KRYSTYNA SKARBEK, or CHRISTINE GRANVILLE, as she was also known, was the Special Operations Executive's

(SOE) longest serving agent during World War II. Polish born to a wealthy noble family, she travelled to England when war broke out and offered her services to the authorities, beginning her undercover work as a courier in Poland. Brave, bold and beautiful, she undertook arduous treks over the Tatra mountains to carry secret mail and money into the country under the code name Madame Marchand, making six journeys over the Polish border and eight over the Slovakian, all of the trips fraught with danger. Her looks and enchanting personality earned her a handful of husbands and scores of admirers – not always convenient when one is an undercover agent, as noted in her file in 1940: "her attractiveness appeared to be causing some difficulty in Budapest and…one of our agents had attempted to commit suicide, first by attempting to throw himself in the Danube which was frozen and secondly by attempting to shoot himself.".

Later in the war she was dropped into southern France and acted as a courier and subverter for SOE there, inducing conscripted Poles to defect. Having survived so many hazardous operations during the war, earning her headlines such as "The ace girl spy on either side in either world war" and "the modern pimpernel no man could resist", she was murdered by a cruise liner steward whom she had rejected, in 1952.

Sir Owen O'Malley: "She was the bravest person I ever knew, the only woman who had a positive *nostalgie* for danger. She could do anything with dynamite except eat it."

Also an agent for the SOE, VIRGINIA HALL relayed infor-

mation from France, where she worked undercover in the offices of the *New York Post*. Previously a member of the diplomatic services, she was forced to end her work for the State Department when she lost her leg as the result of a shooting accident, and had to use a wooden leg, which she called Cuthbert. Later in the war she turned her skills to sabotage, and her achievements included blowing bridges, derailing trains, destroying German lorries and incapacitating phone lines. She was the first woman to be awarded the Distinguished Service Cross.

NOOR INAYAT KHAN was a Sufi princess, born in the Kremlin, on New Year's Day, 1914, who went on to be the first female wireless operator to penetrate occupied France, and was one of only three women awarded the George Cross during World War II. Known as 'Bang Away Lulu' at RAF Abingdon because of her noisy typing, her work in Paris as a radio operator during the summer of 1943 was fraught with danger, as she constantly moved location to avoid detection and worked with little or no support. She was betrayed and arrested, whereupon she immediately tried to escape out of a window, but to no avail.

Despite being held as a 'Night and Fog' prisoner (who were kept in the bleakest cells, in solitary confinement, on minimum rations) and tortured for 10 months, she never talked. She was executed in Dachau concentration camp. Her last word is said to have been 'Liberté'.

VIOLETTE SZABO joined the SOE after the death of her French Legionnaire husband, at El Alamein, and shortly after the birth of their daughter. Said to be the best shot in the SOE, Violette was dropped into Limoges on D-Day, and was captured 3 days later as a result of a German ambush. Her arrest is described by Anastasie Dufour, when she had been injured, and managed to secure his freedom:

"She insisted she wanted me to try and get away, that there was no point in my staying with her...she kept on firing from time to time and [I] managed to hide under a haystack...half an hour later, Szabo was brought to that very farm by Germans; I heard them questioning her as to my whereabouts, and heard her answering, laughing, 'You can run after him, he is far away by now.'"

She was taken to Ravensbrück, where she was executed. Her four-year old daughter, Tanya, later accepted the George Cross on her behalf.

A Cook in the Kitchen

~

MARGUERITE PATTEN'S major contribution to the culinary landscape of Britain was through her wartime work for the Ministry of Food. Her job was to inspire people and teach

them how to eke out the meagre amounts of food available, and she did so with gusto, showing housewives how to create mock cream, eggless sponge and make whale meat palatable.

The author of a staggering 165 books (including the *Spam Cookbook* – Spam soup, soufflé, anyone?) at the time of writing she is still going strong and aged 90.

One of the first 'TV chefs', her programme was initially shown in 1947. But not for her the airs of some of today's gastronomic stars. Josceline Dimbleby says that "When I was organising a charity celebrity's food stall a few years ago the star chefs all got their minions to make things and I told Marguerite I could get someone to make up her jam recipes to save her standing over a hot stove for hours, but she wouldn't hear of it and made it all herself."

LILLA ECKFORD, author of a cookbook now held by the Imperial War Museum and subject of a biography called *Lilla's Feast*, by her great-granddaughter. She wrote her way out of the hellish conditions she found herself in when she was held in a Japanese camp in China, during the Second World War.

She compiled her encyclopaedia of cookery on scraps of paper scrounged from wherever she could, and detailed treats such as honey gingerbread and chocolate layer cake and blancmange, as well as advising women on the equipment necessary for a well stocked kitchen. The thought of her writing recipes for such sweet confections in a dank cell is a touching one.

ELIZABETH DAVID "The single person most responsible for improving British life in the 20th century" according to Auberon Waugh, and the inspiration for many of today's great food writers, Elizabeth David's books have stood the test of time unlike any others, possibly because they are not simply collections of recipes, but lyrical travel writing, social history and manuals for living well too, all written in David's characteristically bossy, headgirl-y tone. Rather scandalously for the time, she spent the wartime years sailing round the Mediterranean with her married lover, before marrying a Lieutenant Colonel in the Indian Army and living with him in India for just a year, before returning to England. It was during the bitter English winter following her return that she started to write her first book, *Mediterranean Food*, which is full of recipes for both classic and more unfamiliar dishes of the region, and vivid descriptions of the flavours of "the bright vegetables, the basil, the lemons, the apricots, the rice with lamb and currants and pine nuts, the ripe green figs, the white ewe's milk cheeses of Greece, the thick aromatic Turkish coffee, the herb-scented kebabs, the honey and yoghurt for breakfast, the rose-petal jam...". Though her influence was not immediate, it has been enduring – she popularised many previously exotic dishes such as hummus, ratatouille and quiche Lorraine, which are now domestic stalwarts.

Foreigners in the Middle East are often heard to complain that they are being served with camel instead of beef. If they had ever eaten camel meat they would soon know the difference.

ELIZA ACTON is an unfamiliar name these days, but deserves a brief mention in this section as the writer of what was probably the first cookbook aimed at the housewife (as opposed to the professional household chef), in which she introduced the now ubiquitous practice of listing the ingredients separately. Previously they tended to be simply mentioned as and when necessary in the body of the recipe. This method was further refined by ISABELLA BEETON, who included many of Eliza Acton's recipes in her *Book of*

Household Management. This monumental volume has sold millions of copies and is by no means just a cookbook. Encyclopaedic in scope, it lists home cures for colds, instructions on 'How to Bleed', quotes passages from other writers, elaborate dinner menus, all manner of inventive ways of coping with leftovers, managing your staff, cleaning stains from silk and ribbons, appropriate conversation, the etiquette of making calls and the rearing of children, as well as information on 'The Disposition of the Turkey' (a peculiar combination of furious and cowardly, apparently) and an entire chapter devoted to 'General Observations on Vegetables'.

Just 23 when she published *Household Management*, Mrs Beeton died in her late twenties in childbirth, but became something of an apocryphal figure because of the lack of announcement of her demise, which led to the popular view of her as a conservative, matronly woman instead of the young and rather innovative woman that she was.

DINNER FOR 18 PERSONS

(For March)

First Course
Turtle or Mock Turtle Soup, removed by
Salmon and dressed Cucumber
Red Mullet
Vase of Flowers
Filets of Whitings
Spring Soup, removed by Boiled Turbot and Lobster Sauce

Entrées
Fricasseed Chicken
Vol-au-Vent
Vase of Flowers
Compôte of Pigeon
Larded Sweetbreads

Second Course
Fore-quarter of Lamb
Braised Capon
Boiled Tongue, garnished
Vase of Flowers
Ham
Roast Fowls
Rump of Beef à la Jardinière

Third Course
Guinea-Fowls, larded, removed by Cabinet Pudding
Apricot Tartlets
Wine Jelly
Rhubarb Tart
Custards
Vase of Flowers
Jelly in glasses
Italian Cream
Damson Tart
Ducklings, removed by Nesselrode Pudding
Cheesecakes

JOSEPHINE COCHRANE was not a cook, and most people will never have heard of her, but will certainly give thanks daily for her invention – the dishwasher. In 1886, suffering from that tedious problem of having servants break too many of her dishes, she stated that "If no one else is going to invent a dishwashing machine, I'll do it myself". And did.

JANE GRIGSON

Although she wrote books on numerous aspects of food and cooking, Jane Grigson may be celebrated as the definitive writer on vegetables. Her book appealed partly because of its friendly, homely tone.

The Vegetable Book *bears the marks of long-term and heroic kitchen carnage. It also bears that other sign of popularity: the insertion of so many newspaper clippings that the book bulges out wider than its own spine. They are there for the simple reason that when Cabbage or Beetroot or Parsnips come to mind, the arm reaches automatically for Grigson, which becomes the obvious repository for the other people's recipes on the same subject.*
Julian Barnes

CLAUDIA RODEN is one of the "food writer's food writers". Her books on Middle Eastern and Jewish food are regarded as definitive. She focuses on home cooking, visiting women cooking for their families in their own kitchens, digging out recipes handed down through the generations, and reproducing them for her readers as faithfully as possible. She aims to do what one Moroccan man proclaimed as being impossible: "How could you possibly communicate in words what my wife has learnt from her mother and her relatives and their cooks, and which she has perfected over fifty years of cooking?" But she does it.

She gets high praise indeed from Simon Schama – "Claudia Roden is no more a simple cookbook writer than Marcel Proust was a biscuit baker. She is, rather, a memorialist, historian, ethnographer, anthropologist, essayist, poet."

∽

CLAUDIA RODEN ON THE WOMEN WHO INSPIRED HER TO COOK

I have always admired and still admire a large number of women in all kinds of fields and for all kinds of reasons. I will only mention those who inspired me to do what I do:

Elizabeth David

Jane Grigson who was also very lovable

Julia Child in the USA

Judith Jones my publisher at Knopf in the USA who must be the best food editor in the world.

Jill Norman who was my publisher and is also a food writer

I had made out a long list of colleagues that I think a lot of, but it was too long and I thought those I left out would be upset.

~

Curry was recently declared to be Britain's favourite food, and **MADHUR JAFFREY** is responsible for creating authentic recipes for it which are accessible and easy to follow. Her calm, friendly style makes the long lists of ingredients less intimidating. This is possibly due to the way she herself learned to cook; having arrived in England to train as an actress she desperately missed the home-cooked Indian food she had grown up with, but had no idea how to cook it, so wrote home to her mother (plaintively telling her 'I only eat chocolate') who began sending her recipes. She writes about the history of the areas her recipes come from, educating her readers on unfamiliar spices and flavours, and is often credited with the increased availability of many such ingredients in the UK.

JULIA CHILD, SIMONE BECK AND LOUISE BERTOLLE– Authors of the seminal and immense text *Mastering the Art of French Cooking*, which contains incredibly detailed instructions on how to create many French classics, including a recipe for French bread that runs to 12 pages. Following from them – **JULIE POWELL** – who undertook to cook every single recipe (even the ones for eggs in aspic) from the above book in just a year, and wrote about it in *Julie and Julia: 365 Days, 524 Recipes, 1 Tiny Apartment Kitchen.*

For every reader who loves to cook and who holds the above

cookery gurus in high esteem, there will be one whose kitchen is the home of a takeaway menu and a fridge for wine, and it is with them that PEG BRACKEN will strike the strongest chord. *The I Hate to Cook Book* is a manual for the domestically challenged, a guidebook through the kitchen trenches. As she says "You don't get over hating cooking, any more than you get over having big feet."

RUTH ROGERS and ROSE GRAY (River Café); ANGELA HARTNETT (The Connaught) – are the only three female head chefs of 100 Michelin starred restaurants in Britain.

CLARISSA DICKSON-WRIGHT and JENNIFER PATERSON toured Britain on their motorbike and sidecar in their successful TV programme *Two Fat Ladies*. Clarissa – full name Clarissa Theresa Philomena Aileen Mary Josephine Agnes Elsie Trilby Louise Esmerelda Dickson-Wright – rages against the trend for vegetarianism and dieting, taking the

view that the downturn in the consumption of animal fats is responsible for the rise in depression. Her appetite for food and life was matched for a number of years only by her appetite for drink – before she stopped drinking she apparently consumed so much gin and tonic that from the tonic alone she developed a rare condition usually only seen in people who have taken a lot of malaria tablets – both contain quinine.

Jennifer Paterson, who died in 1999, cooked the lunches for *The Spectator* magazine, advised the Prince of Wales on organic products, worked as a stage manager, lived in Portugal and Sicily (where Gayelord Hauser turned down lunch with Greta Garbo in favour of Jennifer), and requested caviar, not flowers, to be brought to her in hospital during her last illness.

NIGELLA LAWSON – according to Nigel Slater she is 'the queen of the frozen pea', and her book *How to Eat* does seem to make uncommon use of the humble pea, with 8 recipes for peas in the index, as well as three sections on 'peas for children'. Doyenne of the home kitchen, her recipes always work, and most of them take into account the various constraints of the home cook – fussy children, demanding jobs, mid-week socializing and the need to put on makeup and drink a glass of wine at the same time as cooking the dinner. She also allows for decent sized portions – you never have to double the quantities of a Nigella recipe in order to be confident there will be enough for seconds. Nor does she take food too seriously – a glance over her books reveals:

Peter Rabbit in Mr. McGregor's Salad, green goddess dressing, dolly mixture fairy-cakes, Elvis Presley's fried peanut-butter and banana sandwich, and Love Buns.

"In real life, you can be interested in reading a book and in cooking and in lipstick and in politics – the one doesn't take away from the other."

First Ladies

~

ELEANOR ROOSEVELT, First Lady of the USA from 1933 – 1945, used her time as wife of the President to promote Franklin D. Roosevelt's 'New Deal' and work for increased civil rights, writing a book called 'It's Up to the Women', where she insisted that household servants be paid more fairly. The only First Lady to carry a pistol, she held weekly salons where she served scrambled eggs and called them 'scrambled eggs with brains', and is said to have eaten three chocolate covered garlic balls each morning to improve her memory.

Called the 'First Lady of the World' by some of the media, Eleanor Roosevelt was the first to hold a formal press conference, and was concerned mainly with standing up for her beliefs. She flouted segregation laws, by sitting in between blacks and whites. She was elected as the head of the United Nations Human Rights Commission, but later threatened to resign if President Truman did not recognize the new state of Israel.

"Campaign behaviour for wives: Always be on time. Do as

little talking as humanly possible. Lean back in the parade car so everybody can see the president."

LEGAL AND POLITICAL FIRSTS

MARY MACARTHUR *was the first woman to be nominated as a parliamentary candidate, in 1918.*

The first American Secretary of State was MADELEINE ALBRIGHT, *from 1997 to 2001.*

Post-War defence barrister ROSE HEILBRON *was the first woman to:*

Win a scholarship to Gray's Inn
Be appointed to King's Counsel
Lead in a murder case
Be a 'recorder' (barrister who serves as a part-time Judge)
Sit at the Old Bailey as a judge
Become treasurer of Gray's Inn.

CONDOLEEZZA RICE *is the first African American woman to hold the position of Secretary of State.*

SANDRA DAY O'CONNOR *became the first woman to sit on the Supreme Court of the US in 1981.*

MARGARET THATCHER *was Britain's first female Prime Minister, holding the position from 1979 to 1990.*

The world's first female President was ISABEL PERON, *of Argentina, who served between 1974 and 1976.*

VICTORIA WOODHALL – *the first woman to run for President of the US, in 1872.*

CHERIE BLAIR *was the first, and is still the only person to earn a degree from LSE law school with a first in all her sub-*

jects. Despite the various controversies that have followed her around during her husband's time as Prime Minister, she has fought to find the balance between her personal and public lives, both as the 'First Lady' of the UK, and also as a high-profile human rights lawyer.

EVITA PERON *was the first Argentine woman to campaign publicly, and the first in public life to break the mould by wearing trousers.*

NANCY ASTOR became the first woman MP to take her seat in the House of Commons in 1919. Born in Virginia, she moved to England and married politician and fellow ex-pat, Waldorf Astor. Nancy decided to stand for Parliament after Waldorf inherited his Viscountcy, with the slightly strange campaign slogan 'Vote for Lady Astor and your children will weigh more'. Introducer of the 1923 Private Member's Bill that made it illegal to buy alcohol under the age of 18 she was also an 'ardent feminist', convinced that women had more moral strength than men (who she felt possessed more 'immoral strength'). When she took over the running of Cliveden House upon her marriage to Waldorf, she also established herself as a prominent and influential society hostess, and grande dame of 'The Cliveden Set'. Her dislike of Winston Churchill was well-known and the feeling was mutual.

"'Winston," said Lady Astor to Churchill at a Cliveden breakfast, "if I were married to you I'd put poison in your coffee."

"Nancy," replied Churchill gloomily but with feeling, "if I were married to you, I'd drink it."

~

CHERIE BOOTH'S HEROINES

Dame Cicely Saunders
Eleanor Roosevelt

~

LUCY HAYES was the first President's wife to be called the 'First Lady', by the press, who also named her 'Lemonade Lucy' after she banned alcohol in the White House. The men who served under her husband during the Civil War had the gentler name of 'Mother Lucy' for her, because of her frequent visits to nurse the wounded and talk to the soldiers.

NANCY REAGAN Referred to by the press as 'The First Mannequin' and listed as one of the best-dressed women in America before becoming First Lady, Nancy continued her love affair with designer gowns throughout her stay in the White House. Her passion for designer items wasn't just for frocks – she is said to have bought a set of china in 'a unique shade of red' that is rumoured to have cost more than $1,000 for a dinner plate.

Her nickname is said to be 'Cuddles'.

~

FIRST PHYSICIANS

ELIZABETH GARRETT ANDERSON *was the first female British medic. She was inspired by:*

ELIZABETH BLACKWELL *the first woman in America to be awarded a medical degree, in 1849. Apparently one of her motives for studying medicine was to place a 'strong barrier' between herself and marriage, which seems a rather long way around the problem. But it was all to the greater good, as after the Civil War she and her sister, Emily, went on to work in preventive medicine and establish an infirmary for women in the slums of New York, after the Civil War.*

When Elizabeth first applied to study medicine, her application was accepted only because it was treated as a joke. Many were appalled when they realised it was not, and protested against her being allowed to attend classroom demonstrations. However, she gained her MD, and was presented with it in 1849, in front of 20,000 people.

She later travelled to Britain, where she became the first woman to have her name on the Medical Register, and settled in England, helping to found the London School of Medicine for Women.

MARIA MONTESSORI *was the first woman in Italy to become a qualified physician.*

SHEILA SHERLOCK – *First British Professor of Medicine.*

ELLEN DOUGHERTY, *from New Zealand, became the world's first registered nurse in 1902.*

∽

JACKIE KENNEDY "Queen of America" and a fashion icon whose recognisable style still influences trends today, and who was matriarch of the Kennedy clan whose lives seem charmed and cursed all at once.

She held her country in total thrall – a TV show where she

showed viewers around the White House in 1962 was viewed by three-quarters of the viewing public in America. And she received an Emmy for the programme – the First and Only First lady to do so...

When her personal effects were auctioned at Sotheby's to pay inheritance tax they raised over $30 million, with items going for far more than their material value (a faux-pearl necklace valued at $500-700 sold for $211,500).

The *Evening Standard* said "Jacqueline Kennedy has given the American people…one thing they have always lacked: Majesty."

LOU HOOVER

Apart from some missionaries, Lou Hoover was the first American woman to master Chinese, which she did while she and her husband Herbert travelled to the country at the end of the 19th century seeking gold and coal. She spoke four other languages, and received an award for her work translating manuscripts on mining from the original Latin.

She was also the first First Lady to deliver a radio address, and the first who had earned a graduate degree (geology from Stanford – to add yet another 'first' string to her bow, she was the first ever woman to receive this particular degree in America)

Gave huge, formal dinners at which it has been alleged that the butlers and footmen were selected because they were exactly 5 foot 8.

BETTY FORD A sufferer of breast cancer while in the White House, she spoke openly and frankly about it at a time when the usual practice was not to talk of such matters and went on to do huge amounts of fund-raising for the treatment of cancer. This openness characterises her – she was the first First Lady to admit publicly to problems with alcohol, and she started the Betty Ford Centre in California, spent months fundraising for it, and is its chairwoman. Her work for women's rights has included campaigns for liberalised abortion laws, the appointment of a woman to the US Supreme Court and an Equal Rights Amendment.

HILLARY RODHAM CLINTON. The first First lady to win election to public office as a member of the Senate, she is hotly tipped by some to become America's first woman President. She is probably the Presidential spouse who has had most involvement with politics herself, which has earned her some disapproval, but her active role won her fans as well as critics. She has initiated funding for children's healthcare, and regards the Adoption and Safe Families Act of 1997 as her greatest achievement as First Lady. She acted with quiet if steely dignity during the brouhaha surrounding the revelations of her husband's adultery, and was paid a record $8 million advance for her autobiography.

No woman has yet received a nomination by a major party to run for US Presidency.

FIRST PRIZES

DOROTHY DANDRIDGE *was first black woman to be nominated for an Oscar;* **HATTIE MCDANIEL** *was the first black actress to* win *an Oscar as Best Supporting Actress (for her role as Mammy in* Gone with the Wind*) and* **HALLE BERRY** *became the first black woman to win Best Actress in 2002.*

VIOLET WEBB *was Britain's first woman to win an Olympic medal for athletics, at the 1932 Games in Los Angeles.*

EDITH WHARTON *was the first woman to win the Pulitzer Prize for Fiction, with* The Age of Innocence, *in 1921.*

Seventeen years later, **PEARL S. BUCK** *became the first female winner of the Nobel Prize for literature, with* The Good Earth.

GERTRUDE EDERLE *was the first woman to swim the English Channel in 1926. It took her 14 hours and 39 minutes.*

MARY HEATH *was the UK's first javelin champion.*

BILLIE JEAN KING *is the only player ever to have won US titles on all four surfaces – those being grass, clay, hard court and indoor. She has won 20 Wimbledon titles. And she absolutely thrashed Bobby Riggs in 1973 after he announced that no woman could ever beat him.*

MARTINA NAVRATILOVA *– winner of Wimbledon singles title a record 9 times.*

MARIE CURIE The first person ever to win two Nobel Prizes (for physics and chemistry), she was also the first woman in France to complete her doctorate, and the first (and as yet only) Nobel prize-winning mother of a Nobel prize-winner, after her daughter Irene Joliot-Curie was awarded one in 1935. She remains the only woman to have been awarded the Prize twice.

Along with her husband, Pierre, Marie Curie undertook pioneering work studying radioactive materials. She and her daughter both contracted leukaemia as a result of the high levels of radioactive materials with which they worked (her notebooks apparently are still not safe to handle).

She was also, rather more romantically than you might expect, the focus of a duel between a newspaper editor and an alleged lover. The duel ended with no bloodshed, as neither party fired, but still...

~

The Very First First Lady

Martha Washington

~

FEARLESS FIRSTS

JUNKO TABEI *became the first woman to summit Everest on 16th May 1975.*

ANNIE TAYLOR, *the first woman to go over Niagara Falls in a barrel, in 1901. She was 64 years old at the time.*

ANNIE LONDONDERRY *was the first woman to ride a bicycle around the world, between 1894 and 1895.*

PATRICIA MCCORMICK *was the first professional woman bullfighter, gaining herself two bulls in the contest held in Ciudad Juarez, Mexico, in 1952.*

~

RACHEL ANDERSON is Britain's only licensed female football agent.

Models and Muses

~

SUZANNE VALADON was both an artist herself, and a muse and model to Toulouse-Lautrec, and Renoir (an occupation she took up when her career as a circus acrobat was cut short by injury). She taught herself to draw during the long hours she spent sitting in artists' studios, and became an acclaimed painter in her own right, championed by Toulouse-Lautrec, who introduced her to Degas, who arranged her first exhibitions. She was the mother of Maurice Utrillo, also a painter, and spent much of her later life trying to treat his alcoholism.

KIKI OF MONTPARNASSE was the model for Man Ray's famous photograph depicting her back as a violin, as well as posing for many other artists in 1920s Paris including Alexander Calder and Jean Cocteau. She was named 'Queen of Montparnasse' when she was 28, and performed risqué music hall numbers in black stockings and garters. When she wrote her memoirs they were immediately banned in America, her independent spirit and frank talking proving a little too much for some, including, possibly, Ernest

Hemingway, who said she was 'a woman who was never a lady at any time'...

LORNA WISHART was both an artistic muse and a literary one, as the inspiration for Laurie Lee's *As I Walked Out One Midsummer Morning*, and, later, the model and muse for Lucian Freud. Described after her death, by her daughter, as 'savage, wild, romantic and completely without guilt', and 'a sophisticated mermaid' by her son, she had such an effect on Laurie Lee that he enlisted as a Republican volunteer in Spain to impress her; when she stopped seeing him upon meeting Lucian Freud, he became almost suicidal with longing and misery. In an odd twist, both Freud and Lee later married nieces of Wishart's.

American expat NATALIE CLIFFORD BARNEY reigned over literary Paris at the turn of the 20th century, where she ran a salon, frequented by figures of the era such as Colette, James Joyce, Somerset Maugham, Isadora Duncan, Truman Capote...She is portrayed in many novels of the period, such as *The Well of Loneliness* by Radclyffe Hall and *Claudine and Annie*, by Colette.

She had an affair with SYLVIA BEACH, another Parisian icon, who ran the bookshop *Shakespeare and Company*. This became a centre of literary activity in between-the-wars Paris, with scores of expatriate Americans congregating there. Hemingway, Eliot, Fitzgerald, James Joyce and Gertrude Stein, among others, were all regular visitors to the Left Bank shop.

THE MARCHESA LUISA CASATI was possibly Europe's most eccentric and notorious muse and artist's model. One of the

world's most painted women, she was portrayed by scores of artists, sculptors and photographers. She wore her pet boa constrictor as jewellery, and dressed in opulent, exotic costumes for her legendary parties, at which she would be attended by nude servants covered in gold leaf, and would wander round her gardens wearing only a fur coat, with cheetahs on diamond-studded leads. Almost never out of the gossip columns, she commissioned many portraits of herself, kick-starting many young artists' careers in the process, turning herself into both muse and patron simultaneously. She then housed the paintings in immense galleries in her various palatial homes. But by 1930 she was bankrupt, and her collections were sold off, bought by collectors including Coco Chanel, and Casati relocated to London, where she became involved with a new set of admirers. Her image and style is still influential, decades after her death – she has recently been the inspiration behind Haute Couture collections, a new line of elegant designer clothes named Marchesa after her, exhibitions, films and even a limited edition chocolate truffle.

She died in 1957 and was buried in Brompton Cemetery, with one of her Pekinese dogs lying, stuffed, at her feet.

"The door to the room where we sat chatting suddenly opened. A dead woman entered. Her superb body was modelling a dress of white satin that was wrapped around her like a shroud and dragged behind her. A bouquet of orchids hid her breast. Her hair was red and her complexion livid like alabaster. Her face was devoured by two enormous eyes, whose black pupils almost overwhelmed her mouth painted a red so vivid that it seemed like a strip of coagulated blood. In her arms, she carried a baby leopard. It was the Marchesa Casati."
Gabriel-Louis Pringué

THE DARK LADY, as she is known, was the inspiration for

many of Shakespeare's sonnets, but it is not known who she really was, or even if she ever existed. Various candidates have been proposed and discarded over the years, including one of Elizabeth I's maids of honour, a prostitute, and a man.

INÈS DE LA FRESSANGE was nominated by one contributor as a heroine mainly on the strength of her name and the way it "just rolls off the tongue". Model, muse and mother, her full name is slightly more of a mouthful, but no less wonderful – it is Inès Marie Laetitia Eglantine Isabelle Seignard de la Fressange.

A successful singer in her own right, MARIANNE FAITHFULL will still always be remembered as the girlfriend and muse of Mick Jagger. Photographs of the fragile-looking, beautiful young flower child and the wiry rock star have become part of the imagery that defines the era. Daughter of an Austrian Baroness descended from Baron von Sacher-Masoch, and a British spy, she is said to have inspired the Stones' hit *Let's Spend the Night Together*, among others.

"I am a muse, not a mistress, not a whore."

Model socialite and Superstar of Andy Warhol's film *Poor Little Rich Girl*, among others, EDIE SEDGWICK had a brief and intense friendship with the artist which ended acrimoniously, and she moved on to become the inspiration for Bob Dylan's *Blonde on Blonde* album, and songs such as *Leopardskin Pillbox Hat*. She died of an alcohol and barbiturate overdose in 1971. Other songs about her include *Femme Fatale*, by the Velvet Underground, and *Edie (Ciao Baby)* by The Cult.

The Art of Courage

~

"This is the art of courage: to see things as they are and still believe that the victory lies not with those who avoid the bad, but those who taste, in living awareness, every drop of the good."
Victoria Lincoln, 'The Art of Courage', *Vogue*, Oct 1 1952.

DIAN FOSSEY, author of *Gorillas in the Mist*, lived among mountain gorillas for over 20 years, defending them from poachers and collecting research data on them. It is thought that she was murdered by the poachers she fought, in 1985 and is buried at a site in Rwanda that she created for the burial of dead gorillas.

DAPHNE PEARSON GC was the first woman to be awarded the George Cross, for rescuing a pilot from his burning plane, after it crashed in the grounds of the RAF base where she was working as a medical corporal during World War II. She shielded him with her body, amidst explosions from the bombs on board the aircraft, and returned to the flames in a vain attempt to save the radio operator.

Courageous Characters

Ripley – Aliens
The Duchess of Malfi
Clever Polly – Clever Polly and the Stupid Wolf
Lara Croft
Hermione Granger – *The* Harry Potter *Series*
Clarice Starling – The Silence of the Lambs
Lucy – The Lion, the Witch and the Wardrobe
Nancy – Oliver Twist
Lyra – His Dark Materials
Charlotte Gray – Charlotte Gray
Arietty Clock – The Borrowers
George – The Famous Five

SABRINA SAGHEB, aged just 24, was elected as the youngest female candidate for parliament in the landmark 2005 elections in Afghanistan. She campaigned for an end to forced marriages, and the wearing of the burkha for women to become optional, controversial and dangerous stances in a country where the Taleban threatened to kill any woman who even took part in the election. Seven candidates were murdered before the elections started, and one of Sabrina's co-candidates HOWA ALAM NOORISTANI, was shot four times in an attempted assassination, but was undeterred. Sabrina is also on the national basketball team, and head of the Afghan Basketball Federation.

ABIGAIL WITCHALLS was attacked and left for dead in front of her young son, in an assault near her country home which left her paralysed and unable to speak. After months of treatment, the baby she was in the very early stages of carrying at the time of the attack was born in November 2005. She has become much loved and admired for her seemingly constant smile, and the grace and compassion she has shown during her long convalescence. She has now returned home from hospital, but is still almost totally paralysed.

VIVIAN BULLWINKEL was a 26 year old nurse aboard the SS Vyner Brooke, sailing between Australia and Sumatra in 1942 when it was attacked by Japanese bombers in the Bangka Strait. She made it to an upturned lifeboat where she clung with a group of survivors, and they managed to propel themselves to Bangka Island, which was controlled by the Japanese. She and the other nurses stayed on the beach to look after the injured while the majority of the survivors set off to give themselves up. But soon after they had left the nurses heard gunfire, and, when Japanese soldiers arrived on the beach and ordered them into the water, they knew they were also about to be shot. When the soldiers fired their machine guns into the nurses' backs, Vivian was hit in the leg, but managed to play dead, floating in the water until she was washed back towards the beach. She nursed a surviving soldier and cared for them both before giving herself up and entering a prison camp where she was reunited with some other surviving nurses from the ship. She remained imprisoned there for the next three years. When the war ended Vivian Bullwinkel testified to the Tokyo Tribunal regarding war crimes.

BETTY MOUAT was a spinner and knitter from Shetland, born in 1825, who survived a terrible storm during a boat trip to Lerwick, during which the skipper and crew of the *Columbine* were all drowned. The remote nature of the islands meant that the women who lived there had to be tough, and Betty was no exception. She survived 8 days and 9 nights alone, on a packet of biscuits and a bottle of milk, drifting towards Norway, where she was hauled ashore by local fishermen. Her adventure caught the imagination of many, and was even immortalized in a poem by William McGonagall; "Oh! Heaven, hard was the fate of this woman of sixty years of age/Tossing about on the briny deep, while the storm fiend did rage."

More bravery from the women of Shetland was shown by MAY MOAR and GRACE PETRIE, who both rescued stranded fishermen. May Moar's moment came when the sailor's boat capsized in the treacherous North Sea, and she had herself lowered over a cliff at the end of a rope in order to throw a line to the men, enabling them to come ashore. She was awarded medals for bravery by the RNLI and Royal Humane Society. Grace Petrie, mother of a young child, witnessed a shipwreck from her home in 1856, and rowed out with her elderly father-in-law to rescue the inhabitants of the sinking boat. Grace was also awarded a medal from the RHS.

Another Grace became a well-known seafaring heroine when she rescued 9 soldiers from a shipwreck off the coast of Northumberland in 1838. GRACE DARLING was a lighthouse keeper's daughter when she performed her rescue, and following it, she became a national treasure and something of a celebrity, with countless people requesting locks of her hair and her image on all variety of postcards and gifts.

"'Help! Help!' she could hear the cry of the shipwreck'd crew. But Grace had an English heart, And the raging storm she brav'd; She pull'd away, mid the dashing spray, And the crew she saved.
[The Grace Darling Song]

SOPHIE SCHOLL was a member of a World War II resistance movement called the White Rose Society, a non-violent group who produced anti-Nazi leaflets. After distributing 5 leaflets undetected, Sophie was finally caught when she was spotted by a University caretaker and member of the Nazi party as she dropped another batch of leaflets from the top of a staircase, onto students below. She and the other members of the group were arrested and questioned, before later being found guilty of treason on February 22, 1943. She was beheaded the same day.

LADY GODIVA rode through the streets of Coventry naked, in the 11th century, in order to try and persuade her husband, Leofric, Earl of Mercia, to lift the heavy taxes he had imposed on the city. She agreed to do so, on condition that all the windows in town were shuttered, and all the citizens

remained inside. Everyone did so, apart from the man who is now know as 'Peeping Tom' who, according to the legend was struck blind as he peered through the hole he had drilled in his shutters to get a glimpse of the naked noblewoman…

Damsels in Distress

Penelope Pitstop
Pearl Pureheart
Olive Oyl
Rapunzel
Princess Aurora
Snow White
Betty Boop

PATRICIA MORPHEW was awarded a British Empire Medal for 'conspicuous bravery' for her work driving for the National Fire Service during the Blitz, after she continued to drive to a fire despite her car being hit by a bomb. Described as possessing 'courage a man can envy' by her chief, she calmly doused the flames, and drove the car (on three flat tyres) back to the station, where she requested a replacement car, and went back on duty. During the rest of her shift she put out fires, and removed two incendiary bombs from the upper floor of a building.

ANNE FRANK's *Diary of a Young Girl*, which was written during her 25 months spent in hiding in the back rooms of a grocery in Amsterdam, concealed by a movable bookcase, became one of the most widely read books in the world. In some ways a typical teenage girl, in others, wise far beyond her years, her account of life in hiding, mingled with her hopes and dreams and ambitions, are all the more poignant knowing that she died in a concentration camp after the family was betrayed by an unknown informant.

Her belief that "despite everything, people are really good at heart" represents her status as a martyr, heroine, and a symbol of bravery in the face of unimaginable terror.

FEMALE RECIPIENTS OF THE GEORGE CROSS

BARBARA HARRISON – *An air stewardess awarded the GC for her actions saving others when the plane she was on caught fire.*

Noor Inayat-Khan
Odette Sansom
Violette Szabo

All SOE operatives who were awarded the GC for the bravery in World War II.

No woman has yet been awarded the Victoria Cross.

Where Anne Frank was one of the Jews who went into hiding in the Netherlands, CORRIE TEN BOOM was one of the people who hid them. Along with her family, Corrie helped many Dutch Jews conceal themselves behind a false wall in their home, and helped many more get to other safe houses, until their arrest and incarceration in Ravensbrück concentration camp in 1944. She survived the camp, and spent the rest of her life preaching God's love.

HANNAH SENESH OR SZENES, a Hungarian Jew, escaped to Palestine, but immediately volunteered to return to her country to help others escape. She was arrested not long afterwards, tortured and executed by firing squad in 1944, aged just 23.

> *Found in her cell after her execution:*
> *One – two – three...eight foot long*
> *Two strides across, the rest is dark...*
> *Life is a fleeting question mark*
> *One – two – three...maybe another week.*
> *Or the next month may still find me here,*
> *But death, I feel is very near.*
> *I could have been 23 next July*
> *I gambled on what mattered most, the dice were cast.*
> *I lost.*

Style and Substance

COCO CHANEL

"Nature gives you the face you have when you are twenty. Life shapes the face you have at thirty. But it is up to you to earn the face you have at fifty."

Founder of the renowned couture house Chanel, Coco's influence on fashion and tailoring has been far-reaching, and her trademark collarless jackets and gilt-chain handbags are still seen by many as the epitome of stylish dressing. The only person in fashion to be named as one of *Time Magazine's* "100 most influential people of the 20th century", her best-selling perfume Chanel No 5 is one of the most iconic scents ever, and sells a bottle every 30 seconds.

LULU GUINNESS'S HEROINES

Louise Brooks
Elsa Schiaparelli
Diana Vreeland

One of the most glamorous of the film stars of the 1930s, GRETA GARBO became as famous for her reclusive nature as much as her beauty and her performances.

HELENA RUBINSTEIN

"There are no ugly women, only lazy ones."

Building up her business from 12 pots of face cream which she took to Australia when she emigrated there, the Polish born beautician made enough money to start up salons in London, from which she expanded to become one of the biggest cosmetics companies in the world. Her well-documented rivalry with fellow cosmetics tycoon ELIZABETH ARDEN began when Arden's business manager and ex-husband defected to the Rubinstein camp, a move which understandably enraged his former wife. Elizabeth Arden (born Florence Nightingale Graham) was an enthusiastic racehorse-owner, who was said to insist that her horses be treated with her own skin treatments rather than ones designed for animals.

Completing the triumvirate of female cosmetics giants is ESTEE LAUDER, who started her company in 1946, and whose family still control 90 per cent of it.

CATHERINE DE MEDICI'S commission to a cobbler is the first written record of a high-heeled shoe, created for her to wear to her first Royal Ball. She also invented lip-gloss, by mixing beeswax with food colouring, and her ban on thick waists in her court led to the wearing of tightly-laced corsets by women for over 300 years. Famous during her lifetime for her extravagant and sumptuous banquets at the Palace of Fontainebleau, she was a great patron of the arts.

LAUREN BACALL was discovered by director Howard Hawks' wife, who passed a photo of the then Betty Joan Perske on to her husband. Hawks renamed her and developed what would become her signature pose, with her head tilted to one side and some of her hair over her face. Her first film, *To Have and to Have Not*, gave her both instant stardom and her first husband, Humphrey Bogart. She went on to become one of the most important film actresses of the 20th century, delivering such iconic lines as "You know how to whistle, don't you, Steve? You just put your lips together and blow."

~

Supermodels

Janice Dickinson
Tyra Banks
Claudia Schiffer
Christy Turlington
Linda Evangelista
Naomi Campbell
Kate Moss
Twiggy
Cindy Crawford

Jean Shrimpton
Elle Macpherson
Iman
Jerry Hall
Christie Brinkley
Eva Herzigova
Stephanie Seymour
Yasmin Le Bon
Heidi Klum
Brooke Shields
Niki Taylor

AUDREY HEPBURN has been often called the most beautiful woman of all time, and her elegant, elfin style continues to inspire. Hepburn's performances of Holly Golightly and Eliza Doolittle are iconic, as are her distinctive voice and delivery of lines such as "I'm like cat here, a no-name slob. We belong to nobody, and nobody belongs to us. We don't even belong to each other.", and "Come on Dover, move yer bloomin' arse!"

A victim of the Nazi occupation of the Netherlands as a child, where she is reputed to have helped her mother in her resistance work by delivering messages, she later became a special ambassador to UNICEF, visiting Africa and Asia, and dedicating herself to raising awareness of the living conditions of children in these countries. Married twice and engaged 3 times, she gave her first wedding dress that she was due to wear to marry fiancé James Hanson, to a poor Italian couple who could not afford one.

One of only a handful of performers to have won an Oscar, an Emmy, a Tony and a Grammy award, she spoke five languages, and is said to be the inspiration for the looks of Princess Aurora in *Sleeping Beauty*.

~

ANNABEL GOLDSMITH'S HEROINES

VIOLETTE SZABO

An amazingly brave young Anglo-French girl, married to a Frenchman and living in London during WW2. After the death of her husband at El Alamein she was asked whether she would join the SOE (Special Operations Executive) and willingly volunteered for duty in France with the French Resistance. Having carried out many brave exploits, she was captured after a fierce gun battle whilst giving covering fire to a French Maquis leader. Refusing to reveal any details of her fellow Resistance fighters she was tortured by the Gestapo and finally shot with two others at Ravensbrück. Survivors of this appalling concentration camp described her as outstandingly brave. In 1945, at the end of the war, she was posthumously decorated, the George Cross being presented by the King to her four year old daughter.

Personally I have always been in awe of such courage.

QUEEN ELIZABETH THE FIRST

I believe she was the greatest monarch in English history. When she came to power England was bankrupt and she had to face religious discord. She ruled alone for nearly half a century, one of the most glorious epochs in world history,

She had a great sense of duty, even though it came at great personal cost to her. She was determined to preserve English peace and stability and her love for her subjects was legendary. She was greatly mourned when she died.

MARGARET THATCHER

Not necessarily only for her politics, but for her immense courage in standing up for her beliefs. Politics was very much a man's world in the 1970s and I liked the way in which she refused to give in under pressure, whether it impaired her image or not.

LADY HESTER STANHOPE

She was the niece of William Pitt the Younger and very attractive. She was fascinated by the East and was crowned, according to her own account, Queen of the Desert. She travelled all over what was then called Arabia, which was a very courageous thing to do in the early 19th Century. The internet sums it up better than I can by saying that the East was in her blood and its combination of mystery, romance, mysticism, hardship, fatalism and fanaticism captured her English soul, as it was to capture so many of her countrymen in future decades.

The popular image of CLEOPATRA with black-rimmed eyes and dark hair is enduring. Seemingly something of a cosmetics pioneer, she is said to have coloured her lips with pomegranate seeds, and some say her legendary seductive power was down to her perfume – rose, cardamom and cinnamon oils. She was also credited with writing a book on her beauty secrets.

An important ruler, she inherited a bankrupt kingdom and turned it into the richest in the Mediterranean, establishing successful aqueducts and other engineering projects. During her reign free grain was distributed to the poor when necessary and she founded and maintained peaceful alliances with other countries.

Her relationship with Mark Antony was the inspiration for Shakespeare's play *Antony and Cleopatra*, and they are among history's great lovers.

Beautiful, witty and vivacious, MADAME DE POMPADOUR was the 18th century mistress of King Louis XV of France

who became a leading figure in the courts and social world of the time. She is easily recognisable in portraits because of her enormous, tightly corseted dresses, covered in bows and frills, and her characteristic curled hairstyle which is still known by her name today. Her influence on French architecture can be seen in the Place de la Concorde, on its porcelain industry in rococo gilding and flourishes, and on its champagne glasses, which were allegedly modelled on her breast.

BARBARA HULANICKI opened the first Biba store in 1964, and it quickly became the most popular fashion and lifestyle store of the decade, influencing what young women across the country wore.

"The classic Biba dolly...was very pretty and young. She had an upturned nose, rosy cheeks and a skinny body with long asparagus legs and tiny feet. She was square-shouldered and quite flat-chested. Her head was perched on a long, swanlike neck. Her face was a perfect oval, her lids were heavy with long, spiky lashes. She looked sweet but was as hard as nails. She did what she felt like at that moment and had no mum to influence her judgement."
From *A to Biba*, 1983.

~

Screen Style Icons

Holly Golightly – Breakfast at Tiffany's
Mia Wallace – Pulp Fiction
Satine – Moulin Rouge
Sandy – Grease

Carrie – Sex and the City
Emma Peel – The Avengers
Annie Hall
Catherine Olds Banning – The Thomas Crown Affair
Sylvia – La Dolce Vita
Mrs Robinson – The Graduate

~

Whether or not she can be credited with the invention of the miniskirt is a matter of some debate, but **MARY QUANT** was certainly responsible for its popularisation in this country, along with the patterned and brightly coloured tights she paired the skirts with in her Chelsea shop *Bazaar*. She later launched shiny plastic macs, daring micro-minis and hot-pants, and during her heyday was described as the leading force in fashion outside Paris.

~

Harpers and Queen
Top 20 Most Beautiful Women of the 20th Century

Angelina Jolie
Christy Turlington
Queen Rania of Jordan
Sofia Coppola
Nigella Lawson
Uma Thurman
Emmanuelle Beart
Kate Moss
Aishwarya Rai
Charlotte of Monaco

Charlotte Rampling
Beyonce Knowles
Cate Blanchett
Scarlett Johansson
Ziyi Zhang
Sophie Dahl
Natalie Portman
Liv Tyler
Gisele Bundchen
Jennifer Connolly

DAME VIVIENNE WESTWOOD, queen of punk fashion and the platform shoe is an anarchic force in British design. Her reworking of corsets and crinolines and use of traditional fabrics such as tweed and tartan in unconventional and surprising ways have made her an icon of her trade, and she continues to change and develop her look through her collections.

"You have a much better life if you wear impressive clothes."

Blessed are the Merciful

~

PORTIA, the beautiful heiress in *The Merchant of Venice*, makes the famous 'courtroom speech' when pleading for mercy from Shylock on behalf of Antonio, disguised as a male lawyer.

"The quality of mercy is not strain'd.
It droppeth as the gentle rain from heaven
Upon the place beneath,
It is twice blest:
It blesseth him that gives and him that takes."

When DAME CICELY SAUNDERS opened St Christopher's Hospice, Sydenham, in 1967, she started a revolution in the care of terminally ill patients and pain management, and within the next twenty years, over 150 hospices following her philosophies were opened in Britain. Based on the belief that every human being has the right to 'die well' with dignity and free from pain, her writings on pain relief became used throughout the health service. Initially trained as a Nightingale nurse, in 1997 she was awarded an honorary doctorate of medicine by the Archbishop of Canterbury – the first person in 100 years to receive one, as well as many other medals and awards, and an OBE, DBE and Order of Merit.

ELISABETH KÜBLER-ROSS wrote and campaigned for a more accurate and sympathetic understanding of death and dying, and care for terminally ill patients. She proposed the now generally accepted 'Five Stages' of grief and was a supporter of the establishment of the hospice movement.

"Watching a peaceful death of a human being reminds us of a falling star; one of a million lights in a vast sky that flares up for a brief moment only to disappear into the endless night forever."

MARY SEACOLE was a Jamaican nurse who, upon learning of the Crimean War, applied to become an Army nurse, but was rejected because she was black. Instead of giving up and slinking away, Mary funded her own passage, and set up quarters to nurse officers, and cared for wounded soldiers on the battlefield, where she became known as 'Mother Seacole'. She has, historically, been somewhat overshadowed by:

FLORENCE NIGHTINGALE, who was not only probably the world's most famous nurse, but a statistician of some note, who invented the Pie Chart. Her decision to become a nurse angered her wealthy mother, who would have hoped for a more glamorous society life for her younger daughter. After completing her training she was employed at the 'Institute for the care of Sick Gentlewomen', until the outbreak of the war in Crimea, upon which she travelled with 38 other women to Scutari. Here she found soldiers being treated in appalling conditions, with disease rife and a severe shortage of food and medicines. The situation and number of deaths at Scutari led to her later conviction that cleanliness in hospitals was of the utmost importance, and she became an influential figure in achieving this end, playing an important role in overhauling military hospitals.

DAME SHEILA SHERLOCK, a leading authority on the liver, was also the first woman in this country to become a Professor of Medicine. Whereas the procedure for obtaining samples of the liver had previously been by open surgery, a

procedure that was risky at best for seriously ill patients, she encouraged the use of needle biopsies, making for more accurate, less painful diagnoses. She developed tests which are now used in standard practice, and discovered that hepatitis could be vaccinated against. Elected as a Fellow of the Royal College of Physicians at only 33 (the youngest ever woman to achieve this) she taught a whole generation of liver specialists.

OCTAVIA HILL was one of the driving forces in the establishment of council housing, and of open spaces to be available to the poor. This latter resulted in the establishment of the National Trust, and she served on the Poor Law Commission.

EDITH CAVELL was a nurse in Belgium when First World War broke out, Belgium went under occupation, and the hospital was taken over by the Red Cross. At huge personal risk, and against military law, Edith helped hundreds of soldiers escape into the Netherlands (which was neutral). This led to her being court-martialled by the Germans, during which she refused to admit her actions, and she was executed in 1915. Before she was executed she told the visiting chaplain "I realise that patriotism is not enough, I must have no hatred or bitterness towards anyone."

PRINCESS MARY, PRINCESS ROYAL AND COUNTESS OF HAREWOOD was the daughter of Prince George, born in 1897, and a great grandchild of Princess Victoria. As well as establishing the *Princess Mary's Christmas Gift Fund*, which sent a gift to all British soldiers and sailors at war for Christmas 1914, she trained as a nurse, and went to work at

Great Ormond Street Hospital – a most unusual course of action for a member of the Royal family then, as now.

MARY ANN BICKERDYKE was a hospital administrator and nurse during the American Civil War, who was much loved by the troops and who was utterly dismissive of the official military procedures. A marvellously bossy woman, when an unwitting surgeon attempted to reprimand her, and asked her whose authority she was acting on, she promptly replied "On the authority of Lord God Almighty, have you anything that outranks that?"

CLAIRE RAYNER is one of England's most loved and longest serving agony aunts, with columns in *The Sun* and the *Sunday Mirror*, at one point receiving 1,000 letters a week. She has also been a successful popular novelist, but Claire Rayner first trained as a nurse, and in recent years has become known as a passionate campaigner for the rights of patients in hospitals and against many recent NHS reforms.

One of the most famous and photographed women in the world during her lifetime, an iconic beauty, **DIANA, PRINCESS OF WALES** was dearly loved by millions of people. Her work with AIDS victims had a huge and lasting effect on the way people viewed sufferers – once Diana had been photographed holding the hand of a man in an AIDS ward, attitudes slowly began to change.

President Clinton said of this moment:

In 1987, when so many still believed that AIDS could be contracted through casual contact, Princess Diana sat on the sickbed of a man with AIDS and held his hand. She showed the world that people with AIDS deserve not isolation, but compassion and kindness. It helped change world opinion, and gave hope to people with AIDS with an outcome of saved lives of people at risk.

She would also visit hospices and hospitals alone and unannounced, and sit for hours talking to patients. She was not afraid to go out on a limb for people, to reach out to them.

As an International Red Cross VIP volunteer, she visited Angola and undertook various projects for the campaign against landmines. She was influential in the establishment of the Ottawa Treaty, although it did not go through until after her death, which banned the use of anti-personnel landmines.

Mistresses of Media

~

JANE FONDA is an Oscar winning actress, writer, exercise guru and political activist. Appearances in films such as *Barbarella* made her a famous sex symbol, but she also garnered critical acclaim for her performance in *They Shoot Horses, Don't They?*, in 1969, and she has been nominated for Academy Awards 7 times, winning twice.

But it is screen legend KATHARINE HEPBURN who holds the record for most nominated Best Actress, with 12 nominations and four wins for the coveted title.

JUDY FINNIGAN, half of the king and queen of daytime TV, *Richard and Judy* has become one of the most influential women in the media in Britain today. The team's relaxed style, with Judy rolling her eyes when Richard gets ahead of himself, and firmly putting him in his place, has made her hugely popular with the daytime television audience. And since launching their book club in 2004, the pair have wielded serious power in the literary world, with millions buying their chosen books, and launching the careers of new novelists with the *How to Get Published* competition.

HELEN MIRREN, always beautiful and sexy, has not allowed growing older to hold her back in any way, and proved this by posing naked on the cover of the *Radio Times* for her 50th birthday. First appearing as Cleopatra at the Old Vic in 1965, she went on to become a member of the Royal Shakespeare Company, before moving into film work, where she performed in a variety of, often, overtly sexual roles. She found wider fame in the 1990s with her portrayal of D. I. Tennison in the popular series *Prime Suspect*.

SUE MACGREGOR presented the *Today* programme on Radio 4 for 18 years, becoming one of the country's best known and best loved voices and, according to *The Sunday Times*, "Simply the best female presenter radio has produced".

~

SUE MACGREGOR'S HEROINES

LADY ANNE BARNARD, *the wife of the colonial secretary to the Cape of Good Hope in the 1790s, who wrote letters and a wonderful diary describing life in the Cape. They show a sharply observant eye and a good wit. She also climbed Table Mountain in late middle age and a long skirt.*

HELEN SUZMAN, *for many years the lone scourge in parliament of the old white Nationalist government in apartheid South Africa. She was extremely determined and brave, and was one of Nelson Mandela's special guests of honour at his Presidential inauguration in 1994.*

JULIE WALTERS, *a wonderful actress who has known difficult times in her personal life. No-one for me has quite the same ability to translate comedy or tragedy in such an intensely affecting way. She certainly makes me laugh like no-one else.*

⁓

ANNA WINTOUR is editor in chief of *Vogue* magazine and, as such, one of the most influential people in magazines and fashion today. In her role as editor she has nurtured young designers, as well as more established names, and opened beauty salons in Afghanistan after the fall of the Taliban.

JILL DANDO became one of the BBC's most familiar and popular faces because of her considerable skills as a presenter, fronting *Crimewatch*, reading the news and also working on lighter shows, such as *Holiday*, until her shocking murder in 1999. *The Jill Dando Institute of Crime Science* has since been established in her name.

GLORIA HUNNIFORD was the first woman to have her own daily show on Radio 2, and has presented and appeared on many other radio and television shows, winning several prestigious awards for her work. Since the death of her daughter, Caron Keating, from cancer, she has established a foundation in Caron's name to support people affected by the illness and offer support to carers and practitioners.

No woman has ever won the Oscar for 'Best Director'

Saints and Seers

JOAN OF ARC

Joan of Arc had been experiencing visions and visitations from the Archangel Michael since she was 12 years old, but it was not until she was 16 that she was told by him to leave her village to go and help fight the battle against the English. She went to the Dauphin, told him she had been sent by God to aid him, and, once his theologians were convinced that she was telling the truth, he had a suit of armour specially made for her, and sent her off to lead a troop of soldiers to Orleans.

She took fortress after fortress, aided by her men and the zeal of the righteous, including the 'impregnable' Les Tourelles, and went on to Rheims, and the crowning of the Dauphin. By now she was a true heroine, hugely popular and influential, but this was not to last for long. After Charles VII signed a treaty with the Duke of Burgundy, against Joan's wishes, things began to go badly wrong. She was injured by a cross-bow bolt, her page was killed in battle, and her famous and symbolic sword was broken, a mishap that was seen by her superstitious troops as a Sign. Some of her soldiers began to ignore Joan's orders, and she was eventually taken prisoner by a citizen of Burgundy, who sold her to the English.

Despite the outcry of the French people to save her, Charles refused to pay any ransom for her, as did the Church and the City of Orléans. She failed in an attempt to escape, knocking herself unconscious as she fell from a tower. She appeared in court representing herself, to answer the scores of charges against her. In the end, the only charge she was convicted of was the wearing of men's clothes, but nevertheless, for this she was burned at the stake in the marketplace in Rouen.

ALEXANDRA DAVID-NEEL walked to Lhasa, disguised as a begging Tibetan pilgrim, in order to become the first Western woman to visit the centre of Buddhism, usually a world closed to outsiders. The author of various serious books of Buddhist scholarship, she was also, in 1911, the first Western woman to ever gain an audience with a Dalai Lama. Her journey to Lhasa took four years and required huge amounts of determination and perserverance, as she travelled through Burma, Japan and across China and into Tibet on the back of a mule, a yak, a horse, and eventually by foot, any exposed skin covered with soot to disuise her race, through unmarked trails and snow-covered mountain passes. She arrived in Lhasa in time for the spectacular New Year celebrations, with huge pageants full of drums and flags and dancing. She died aged 100 in 1969.

JULIAN OF NORWICH was a 14th century mystic who wrote her *Sixteen Revelations of Divine Love* after experiencing a series of visions of the Passion, the Virgin Mother and the Holy Trinity, following a serious illness. The book is one of the most important documents of its kind (possibly the first work written in English by a woman) and is still highly regarded as a work of Christian devotion and a guide to prayer today. From it comes the famous saying "All shall be well, and all shall be well, and all manner of thing shall be well."

HILDEGARD OF BINGEN was a musical mystic, who, as well as writing on various subjects including natural history, descriptions of her visions and scientific works, wrote the earliest surviving Mass composed by a woman. This was part of a large body of compositions written for performance by nuns and monks in their orders. An unusually eloquent, powerful and well-travelled woman for her time, Hildegard also wrote academic treatises on medical and natural sciences. She had a keen interest in languages, and invented an alternative alphabet and her own language.

SAINT MARGARET CLITHEROE, sometimes known as 'The Pearl of York' became a martyr when she refused to stand trial for the charges of harbouring Catholic priests during the 16th century, because if she did her children would have to testify. Because of this she was crushed to death (the usual punishment for such a crime at the time) on Good Friday, 1586.

Mightier than the Sword

~

"They sicken of the calm, who knew the storm."
Dorothy Parker, *Fair Weather*, 1928

With her witty and often biting social commentary, and sharply humorous verses, **DOROTHY PARKER** was one of the leading members of New York's *Algonquin Round Table*, a group of journalists and writers who met for lunch in the fashionable hotel in the years following World War I.

Unfortunate Coincidence

By the time you swear you're his,
  Shivering and sighing,
And he vows his passion is
  Infinite, undying –
Lady make a note of this:
  One of you is lying.

~

Nobel Prize for Literature Winners

Selma Lagerlof – 1909
Grazia Derledda – 1926
Sigrid Undset – 1928
Pearl Buck – 1938
Gabriela Mistral – 1945
Nelly Sachs – 1966
Nadine Gordimer – 1991
Toni Morrison – 1993
Wislawa Szymborska – 1996
Elfriede Jelinek – 2004

~

JANE AUSTEN wrote *Pride and Prejudice* when she was just 21. It was her first novel, and not published until 6 years later, when it appeared anonymously. Austen did not have serious success, either critical or financial, until after her death – in fact she wrote in secret for much of her life. The combination of Austen's poor health and her refusal of a proposal of marriage from a wealthy man meant that she never moved out of her family home. Having made her decision, it seems likely, at least from some of her novels, that she questioned whether it had been the right one. Her writing is witty and astute, she wrote of the complex system of manners and morals which characterised her era, placing such issues within the framework of touching love stories.

J. K. ROWLING is famous not only for her invention of the

world of Harry Potter, but for the much repeated story of how her first book was written – at a corner table in cafes while her infant daughter slept. Single-handedly, with this series, she has encouraged a generation of children all over the world to read. Her wealth has recently been estimated at $1 billion, by Forbes.

Extraordinarily prolific children's writer ENID BLYTON did exactly the same for an earlier generation, in spite of the opposition of many parents who thought her books were blandly written. Stories such as those about *The Magic Faraway Tree*, *The Famous Five*, and the boarding school *Malory Towers* series, sold in their hundreds of thousands and continue to sell. Blyton's output is estimated at around 600 titles.

Pulitzer Price for Fiction Winners

Harper Lee – To Kill A Mockingbird
Shirley Ann Grau – The Keepers of the House
Katherine Ann Porter – Collected Stories
Jean Stafford – Collected Stories
Eudora Welty – The Optimist's Daughter
Alice Walker – The Color Purple
Alison Lurie – Foreign Affairs

Toni Morrison – Beloved
Anne Tyler – Breathing Lessons
Jane Smiley – A Thousand Acres
E. Annie Proulx – The Shipping News
Carol Shields – The Stone Diaries
Jhumpa Lahiri – Interpreter of Maladies
Marilynne Johnson – Gilead
Geraldine Brooks – March

Iconic poet and novelist SYLVIA PLATH struggled with depression and mental illness throughout her life, writing about her breakdown in her novel *The Bell Jar*. She married fellow poet Ted Hughes in 1956, but the marriage was a turbulent one, and they later separated. She became the first poet to be awarded the Pulitzer Prize posthumously for a collected edition of her poetry. Plath committed suicide in 1963, and since her death has become an almost mythical figure. Whether this is as a result of her writing, her personal life, the manner of her death, or, more likely, some combination of all three, she continues to inspire and touch those who read her.

The first real blockbuster, *Peyton Place*, was written by GRACE METALIOUS, and published in 1956. Its portrayal of sex, secrets and scandal in small town America caused mass shockwaves when it appeared, and this probably contributed to its huge success – it stayed on the bestseller lists for over a year, and permanently changed America's publishing industry.

SUSAN HILL'S HEROINES

VIRGINIA WOOLF *Not only a genius, a great novelist and critic; she set up (with her husband) her own publishing company, the Hogarth Press, did the printing and packed the parcels.*

PENELOPE FITZGERALD *She was a great novelist and one of the most modest, humble, courteous and gracious of women.*

MARILYN MONROE *The woman with the most X factor of any. Beauty, humour, talent, grit, a figure to die for – and yet one whose life was a tragedy from beginning to end.*

BASIA ZARZYCKA *Design genius, creator of wonderful, exotic, beautiful fantasy clothes which are wearable too, and absolutely unlike those of any other designer.*

DOLLY PARTON *The songs, the voice, the accent, the one-liners, the clothes, the hair, the fingernails…*

CAROLE BAMFORD *For working her butt off to create the unique Daylesford organic empire when she is rich enough to do nothing but Lunch every day.*

THE QUEEN *She is dedication personified, she is indefatigable, she is a role model for what to look like when you are eighty, and she makes very droll off the cuff remarks – people forget. She also defies the Health and Safety police by refusing to wear a crash hat when riding which is foolish but feisty.*

George Eliot

Author of *Middlemarch*, *Adam Bede* and *The Mill on the Floss*, among others, her books are much loved for their intricately portrayed characters.

She insisted upon living her life the way she wished, regardless of contemporary opinion. She was disowned not once but twice by her family. She 'lived in sin' with a married man and later married her young lover. And she was famously ugly, yet did not let this hold her back – Henry James said of her: "She is magnificently ugly, deliciously hideous...In this vast ugliness resides a most powerful beauty which, in a very few minutes steals forth and charms the mind, so that you end as I ended, in falling in love with her. Yes, behold me in love with this great horse-faced bluestocking."

Eponymous Heroines

Lorna Doone
Zuleika Dobson
Anna Karenina
Lolita
Rebecca
Moll Flanders
Clarissa
Jane Eyre
Nana
Mrs Dalloway
Madame Bovary

ADÈLE GERAS'S HEROINES

HELEN OF TROY

I've been preoccupied with Helen and her cousin, Penelope (see below) for the last six years, as they've both been characters in books I've written. I first met them aged six reading Tales of Troy *by Andrew Lang. I think Helen was kind, highly intelligent and sophisticated. Her libido got her into trouble, her beauty was a problem, and I think she dealt with it rather shrewdly.*

PENELOPE

The wife of Odysseus is generally cast as the goody-goody but I've always suspected there's more to Penelope than meets the eye. Just because you're not as beautiful as Helen of Troy doesn't mean you are not good-looking, and having a reputation for fidelity doesn't rule out temptation. I also very much admire her weaving skills.

JANE EYRE

The archetypal plain, small, undistinguished heroine who triumphs and gets her man and learns a great deal about life and herself. I admire Jane's tenacity, humanity and bravery and her narrative voice makes the novel what it is.

JO MARCH

Almost every woman writer says she wanted to be Jo when she was a girl. Little Women *is my top children's book of all time and I identify with Jo completely.*

EMILY DICKINSON

Because I love her poems and am deeply attracted to the story of her life and the image I have of her....in a white dress, always.

MARIA CALLAS

Her life reads like the most dramatic of dramas. It's full of tragedy, anguish, betrayal, loss...and I identify with her fight to lose weight. Her voice is what I think of when I think 'opera'.

ROSA LUXEMBURG

A great thinker and revolutionary who was deeply involved in the political upheavals of her time. She was a devoted friend and lover, and adored her cats. She wrote the most wonderful letters from prison, and her death was both tragic and dramatic.

ELIZABETH FRY

Prisons are my idea of hell. They are dreadful places and Fry worked tirelessly to make conditions better in gaol. She was a Quaker and very much ahead of her time. I admire her enormously.

COLETTE

She is a heroine because of the beauty of her prose. She brings the physical world alive like no one else and she, too, was a cat-lover. She was very good at delineating relationships, especially between lovers, and between mothers and children. She understood the human heart.

BILLIE HOLIDAY

She's amazing. Her life story is tragic and you can't listen to her songs without weeping. There isn't a more recognizable voice in the whole of music and it goes straight to your soul.

JUDY GARLAND

Another great singer. She only got hooked on drugs because of her lifelong struggle with her weight. I grew up thinking

I could be exactly the same sort of singer. I know I could never be Billie Holiday, (see above) but I did for a long time aspire to Judyness.

Jane Austen

Her novels are the very best and they change with the age of their reader. Pride and Prejudice *read at 16 is not the same book when you come back to it in your sixties. I like also her modesty: the story of how she hid her work when someone came into the room by pushing it under a mat at the table appeals to me. I also greatly admire precisely what her detractors hate...who says she has to write about the Napoleonic Wars?*

Mrs Gaskell

She's the novelist I'd most like to have round for tea. I'm sure she'd have been terrific company. I like the fact that she integrated her work into her life in a seamless way, and turned her hand to every sort of writing. Best of all is the quality that Virginia Woolf, I think, noticed. She said that Mrs Gaskell wrote as though there were a cat on her lap. Quite so. Fantastic! Catlap writing produced some really wonderful books.

∽

Virginia Woolf

One of the greatest novelists of the 20th century, Virginia Woolf has since the 1970s, become an icon for feminists. She suffered from bouts of both mental and physical illness all her life but she was nevertheless tough and hard-working, not only as a novelist but as a prolific literary critic and essayist. She also, with her husband Leonard Woolf, founded the Hogarth Press, and not only selected and edited the titles they published, but installed a printing press in their dining room and learned to print, fulfilled orders and packed parcels.

She has been claimed as a lesbian because she fell in love and ran away with Vita Sackville West, but the affair was more of an emotional drama than a fully-fledged union – Virginia was uninterested in sex. But she and Leonard had a long and supremely happy marriage, based on close friendship, shared interests, a comfortable domestic life and many friends.

Fearing the onset of another bout of mental illness, Virginia Woolf committed suicide by drowning in 1941.

CARMEN CALIL founded the Virago Press in 1972, with the aim of publishing books by women, and later the Virago Modern Classics, which brought forgotten and languishing works back into the mainstream. They rediscovered works such as *Testament of Youth* and *The Women's Room*, and continue to publish classics and new writers, and were the first publishers in the UK of MAYA ANGELOU, who has inspired millions of women with her autobiographical accounts of rape, abuse and hardship in the Depression years. Angelou is an important Civil rights figure, campaigning for equality, and has been awarded more than 50 honorary degrees.

No woman has held the post of Poet Laureate.

Wives and Mothers

GLADYS AYLWARD, an English-Chinese missionary who spent many years living in southern Shanxi preaching the gospel led 100 children on a mountain march out of the area when war with the Japanese reached the area in 1938. Some of them were children she had bought from beggars who were using them to gain sympathy and more money, others orphans that she had gathered along the way.

MARGE SIMPSON

Heroic by anyone's standards for putting up with Homer, Marge is perhaps the ultimate role model for today's housewife, mother, or indeed any woman. She has worked as a Roller-skating waitress, Pretzel maker, Police Officer, Tradeshow model, Estate Agent, Springfield Nuclear Power Plant Worker, Actress, Artist, Substitute teacher, Novelist, Church counsellor, Bodybuilder, Chief cook for Hell's Satan's biker gang.

MARY POPPINS, the ultimate nanny, for being superfragilisticexpialidocious.

Famous Mothers

Mother Theresa
Mother Goose
Whistler's Mother
Mother Jones
Grandmother Moses
Queen Elizabeth, the Queen Mother
Old Mother Hubbard
The Virgin Mary

EGLANTYNE JEBB and her sister DOROTHY BUXTON founded the Save the Children Fund after the First World War, in order to obtain famine relief for the millions of children affected by the war. She raised huge amounts of money to this end, and later expanded the remit of the charity to other issues in children's rights. Her *Declaration of the Rights of the Child* was accepted by the UN in 1924. She died in 1928.

CAROLE HALL was named Inspirational Mum of the Year by *Tesco Magazine* in January 2006. A foster mother from Ipswich, she has fostered 300 children over a period of 16 years.

Wives

The Stepford Wives
The Merry Wives of Windsor

THE SIX WIVES OF HENRY VIII

CATHERINE OF ARAGON, Henry's first wife, whose marriage to him was annulled, despite their having an apparently harmonious union, on the grounds that she had previously been married to his brother. The true reason was that although she had given birth to six children, the only surviving child was a daughter, and Henry wanted a son and heir. The Pope refused to annul the marriage, and so Henry created an Act of Parliament allowing him to divorce her, in 1533, and marry ANNE BOLEYN, in a move which led to England's separation from the Roman Catholic Church and eventual establishment of the Church of England.

ANNE BOLEYN gave birth to the future Elizabeth I shortly after their marriage, but also failed to provide a son, and Henry accused her of adultery and treachery, and imprisoned her in the Tower of London. In 1536 five men (including her brother) who stood accused of being her lovers were executed, and she followed them two days later.

She was succeeded by one of her ladies in waiting, JANE SEYMOUR, who did manage to bear a son, the prince who would become Edward VI, but she died shortly after his birth.

Henry's fourth marriage, to ANNE OF CLEVES, lasted only

six months, and was annulled in July 1540, on grounds of non-consummation.

Next, he moved on to another Catherine, and cousin of his second wife, CATHERINE HOWARD. However the huge age gap (he was 49 and she just 15 or 16) was probably a contributing factor to her infidelity with Thomas Culpeper, and upon discovering this betrayal, Henry lost no time in having them both executed.

A year later he married his sixth and final wife, CATHERINE PARR, becoming her third husband, and the marriage lasted for four years, until Henry's death in 1547.

High Flyers

~

"Had I been a man, I might have explored the poles or climbed Mount Everest, but as it was, my spirit found outlet in the air."

AMY JOHNSON completed the first woman's solo flight from London to Australia (17 days) in a Gypsy Moth. Setting off from Croydon, she landed in Vienna, then Istanbul, flew over the desert and through sandstorms to Baghdad, then on to Karachi, establishing a new record for flying time from Britain to India. Her plane suffered some damage around Rangoon, but had attracted plenty of interest by the time Amy landed in Singapore, and on her arrival in Darwin she was famous and received congratulations from the King and Queen, along with a CBE. She also flew solo from London to India and Tokyo, and was the first woman to fly the Atlantic from East to West. Ironically, given the long flights she had survived previously, she disappeared on a short flight over the Thames Estuary, and the circumstances of her death are surrounded by rumour and mystery – was she flying a spy out of the country? Shot down by anti-aircraft guns? Was her death faked? None of these stories have ever been substantiated, and her body has never been found.

BARONESS RAYMONDE DE LA ROCHE of France became the first licensed woman pilot in 1910.

BARBARA HARMER was the world's only female supersonic pilot when she was Senior First Officer for the Concorde fleet. Having left school at 15 to become a hairdresser in Bognor Regis, she went on to become an air traffic controller, and studied part time for her A-levels, before going on to gain her pilot's licence.

AMELIA EARHART racked up quite a collection of aviation firsts and records. First woman to cross the Atlantic (as a passenger), first non-stop flight from Mexico to New Jersey, and Hawaii to California, first woman to cross the Atlantic solo, first woman to fly solo non-stop coast to coast, piloted the first civilian plane to carry a two-way radio, first to fly from the Red Sea to India...

She set, broke, and broke again speed and altitude records, and describes drinking a thermos of hot chocolate, on her flight from Honolulu to California – "Indeed, that was the most interesting cup of chocolate I have ever had, sitting up eight thousand feet over the middle of the Pacific Ocean, quite alone."

In 1928 she became the first woman pilot to fly solo across the United States and back. Her first stop was in Bellefonte, Pa., where she was treated to her favourite lunch of fried eggs and ham.

[In 2001 CARLENE MENDIETA recreated this journey in an antique Avro Avian plane, dressing in clothes of the period and staying in the same hotels, and eating the same meals along the way, in a tribute to AE]

Her plane disappeared in 1937 in an attempt to fly around the world, during which she planned to document the effects of flight on the human body. Neither the body of AE nor her navigator has ever been found. The American government spent $4million searching for her – the most money spent on an air and sea search at the time, but with no success. There has been ongoing speculation as to what happened to her, with claims that she was captured by the Japanese, among other, wilder theories. None of these have been backed up by any serious evidence.

"Please know that I am quite aware of the hazards. Women must try to do things as men have tried. When they fail, their failure must be but a challenge to others."
Letter to her husband before her last flight, received by him after her death.

"KHAQQ calling Itasca. We must be on you, but cannot see you. Gas is running low."
Last radio communiqué before she disappeared.

MADAME ELISABETH THIBLE – First woman to make an untethered flight of any kind, in a hot air balloon in Lyons, in 1784, singing an aria.

KATHERINE STINSON – First woman to fly the mail, in 1913. She was thrown out of her plane and killed.

CARLOTTA MYERS rose 21,000 feet – or four miles, in a hot air balloon, with no oxygen or special equipment, in 1886. Amazingly, she survived with no apparent ill-effects. She was married to an aeronautical navigator and inventor, and they lived in a mansion known as The Balloon Farm.

The Powder Puff Derby, in 1929, was a transcontinental race entered by 20 women flyers, which took 8 days to fly. 14 women completed the first derby:

Louise Thaden (winner)
Amelia Earhart
Ruth Elder
Edith Foltz
Mary Haizlip
Jessie Keith-Miller
Opal Kunz
Blanche Noyes
Gladys O'Donnell
Phoebe Omlie
Neva Paris
Thea Rasche

Bobbi Trout
Mary von March
Vera Dawn Walker

DOLLY SHEPHERD was a celebrated exhibition parachute jumper around the turn of the century for 8 years, surviving a tandem jump that went wrong when her partner's parachute failed to open, until she had a premonition that if she made another jump it would be her last. She never jumped again.

E. LILLIAN TODD, First woman to design a plane in 1906.

A Bible, a shotgun, tennis rackets, two silk dresses, an evening gown and a pair of black satin shoes, six pairs of silk stockings, a pair of goggles and a fur coat, but only one change of underclothes. These were allegedly the items deemed essential by LADY MARY HEATH, 'Queen of the Skies', for her flight from Cape Town to London – she was the first pilot to complete this flight, and it took her three months to do so. She claimed that flying was so safe that a woman could "fly across Africa wearing a Parisian frock and keep her nose powdered all the way".

She also spent 2 years working as a dispatch rider during World War I, married three times, was Britain's first javelin champion, the first British woman to hold a commercial flying licence, the first woman to parachute from an aeroplane, when she landed in the middle of a football match, and later becoming the first woman to gain a mechanic's qualification in America. She achieved all this despite an unhappy early family life – her father bludgeoned her mother to death, and was imprisoned for life.

"She made the wings fast in flying position, climbing around the plane like a great cat. She was clad in a colorful cretonne smock and wore high, soft leather boots ...She spun the propellor and started the engine herself while a score of men and boys stood open-mouthed in a semi-circle."
The Jacksonville Journal

JACQUELINE COCHRAN held more aviation speed records than any other woman. Awarded the Harmon Trophy as most distinguished aviator of the year 6 times, she became the only living woman in the American Aviation Hall of Fame in 1971. She was the director of the Women's Auxiliary Service Pilots during World War II, and was the first woman to break the sound barrier, in a Sabre Jet in 1953.

FLORENCE 'PANCHO' BARNES

'When you have a choice – choose happy'

Founder of *The Pancho Barnes Flying Mystery Circus of the Air*, Pancho rode a mule over 1000 miles through Mexico, during a revolution, disguised as a man. Born on millionaire's row in Pasadena, she grew up in a thirty-five room mansion with butler and servants, a pony at the age of 3 and a swimming pool. She obtained her pilot's licence in 1912 and performed elaborate stunts at air shows, such as dropping a roll of toilet paper from the cockpit and following it down with the plane in spirals

On only her second ever solo flight she piloted the plane while her passenger wing-walked. She worked as a test pilot and a stunt pilot in films before starting the Women's Army Reserve, to provide aid during national emergencies.

Her 'Happy Bottom Riding Club' was staffed entirely bywaitresses with the surname Smith, because Pancho thought it seemed mysterious.

Evelyn 'Bobbi' Trout

Set a spread of refuelling endurance world records, in partnership with Elinor Smith, staying in the air for 122 hours.

The world's first licensed African American pilot and only the 2nd black pilot, BESSIE COLEMAN, had to travel to France to get her licence, because of the lack of opportunities for a black woman in America.

SALLY RIDE was the first American woman to fly in space, in 1983.

VALENTINA TERESHKOVA became the first woman to fly in space in 1963 aboard the Soviet spacecraft Vostok 6. She was named Greatest Woman Achiever of the Century in 2000 by the International Women of the Year Association. She is still the only woman who has carried out a solo space flight for 3 days, and has a moon crater named after her.

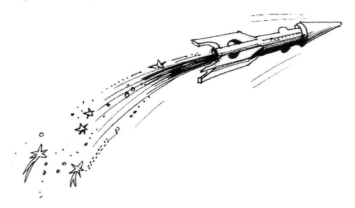

HELEN SHARMAN became the first Briton in space aged just 27. Previously a chemist working for Mars confectionery, she was selected from 13,000 applicants to be the British member of Project Juno after answering a radio advertisement that stated:

Astronaut wanted. No experience necessary.

She spent 18 months training near Moscow for the mission, during which time she became fluent in Russian, before going into quarantine in Kazakhstan for two weeks and eventually spending 8 days in space, carrying out a variety of scientific experiments.

ELLEN CHURCH was the first airline hostess, in 1930.

MADAME SOPHIE BLANCHARD became the first woman to die in a balloon when giving a fireworks display over the Tivoli Gardens in Paris.

JESSIE WOODS and her husband founded The Flying Aces Air Circus, and Jessie was a pioneering wing-walker, who also parachuted and performed gymnastics from a rope ladder suspended from the planes.

Another death-defying wing-walker was GLADYS INGLE, who was famous for firing arrows at a target while balanced on the top wing of a plane, and also for plane-changing mid-air.

PEARL CORNIOLEY was the leader of 1,500 French freedom fighters during World War II and was presented with her 'wings' by the RAF in 2006, at the age of 92. The wings are presented to parachutists who have carried out a certain number of jumps, but as she had not been allowed to make as many (because of her sex) she had never received them. She was parachuted into France at an altitude of just 300 feet, and worked there for the Special Operations Executive as a courier, and later helped run the 'Wrestler' movement which aimed to hinder German movements prior to the D-Day landings, for which she had a 1 million franc bounty put on her head by the Nazis. She was recommended for a Military Cross but because she was a woman was not eligible, and when offered the MBE she turned it down as mere 'decoration'.

CAROLYN GRACE is the world's only female spitfire pilot.

High Flyers with their feet on the ground

OPRAH WINFREY is a powerhouse of achievement, as a philanthropist, a businesswoman, an actress and producer, a publisher.

A born orator, Oprah was speaking in church from the age of 3, speaking the sermons of James Weldon Johnson all over Nashville. *The Oprah Winfrey Show* debuted in 1986, with an episode called 'How to Marry the Man or Woman of Your Choice'. The programme has never shied away from controversy, or difficult subjects, with Oprah confronting people from a county where no blacks had lived for over 75 years (and the residents were keen to keep it that way), meeting a mayor who had ordered a town swimming pool closed after a resident with HIV swam in it, women accused of murder, and a bestselling format of ordinary people with extraordinary stories – mothers of septuplets, bigamists, sufferers of multiple personality disorder, and lots of weight loss and abuse stories.

She has been at the forefront of the campaign against child abuse, and for the rights of women the world over. In 1993 the Oprah Bill, which established a national database of child abusers was signed into law by President Clinton. Information on this Bill is available to law enforcement agencies US wide, and it aims to protect children from abuse. Her 'Angel Network' has raised millions of dollars and supports women's shelters and youth centres, and established schools and scholarships.

She was the First African-American woman to become a billionaire.

Forbes' Top Ten Most Powerful Women

Condoleezza Rice
Wu Yi
Yulia Tymoshenko
Gloria Arroyo
Margaret Whitman

Anne Mulcahy
Sallie Krawcheck
Brenda Barnes
Oprah Winfrey
Melinda Gates

MADAME C. J. WALKER was America's first female millionaire, quite a feat for a black girl from the South who was orphaned at six years old. After attending the World Fair in 1904, she developed a range of cosmetics and hair products for African-American women, including Wonderful Hair Grower.

She later opened the Walker College, and taught hundreds of women the skills necessary to earn a living as a hair dresser, and so work their way out of poverty. "I am not satisfied in making money for myself," she said at a 1914 convention of the National Negro Business League. "I endeavour to provide employment for hundreds of the women of my race." And during the 78 years that her company traded, a woman was always at the helm.

TAMARA MELLON MD of Jimmy Choo, who has built the brand up from a small and little known one into a global phenomenon valued at around £100 million.

"I may not have the stereotypical head for business, but I have feet that were made for heels."

~

SALLY GUNNELL'S HEROINES

STEFFI GRAF
A determined lady coping well under pressure on and off the court and this is proven by the length of her career and the tennis titles she won.

MADONNA
A strong and talented lady who never gives up even when everyone seems to be against her. She is an unmistakable genius of reinvention. And projects a good work – life balance.

DIANNE THOMPSON CBE, Camelot chief executive
A strong determined women in a man's world. To quote Diane 'So do I think I am having a tougher time … yes I do but can I complain – no!' – Finance Mail, Women's Forum. Dec '02

~

CHRISTIE HEFNER is the Chairman of Playboy Enterprises, and, since taking over from her father Hugh, has built up and consolidated the company's international and media presence. She made *Playboy* the first magazine to successfully break onto television, and the first national magazine to

have an internet presence. Highly acclaimed for her work in increasing the amount of opportunities for women in business and female entrepreneurs, she has received the Eleanor Roosevelt Award for humanitarian work and been named as one of the hundred most powerful women in the world.

All-Singing, All-Dancing

~

"*Remember,* GINGER ROGERS *did everything Fred Astaire did, but she did it backwards and in high heels.*"
Faith Whittlesey

GINGER ROGERS has hundreds of film and television credits to her name (as well as five husbands) but it was her partnership with Fred Astaire in films such as *Flying Down to Rio, Shall We Dance*, and *Top Hat*, which shot her to fame. Scores of Gershwin classics came from these films, and the sweeping costumes and longing looks shared by Rogers and Astaire still capture our imagination today as strongly as they did in the bleak years of the Depression.

THE SPICE GIRLS shot to worldwide fame in 1996 with "Wannabe" and continued to reign supreme over the British charts for the next 4 years. Their cutesy, infectious pop and bubblegum philosophy of Girl Power made them the heroines of millions of girls, and their cleverly branded image made them the fantasy of both teenage boys and marketing men everywhere. They were the biggest selling female group of the 20th century, and they were:

Victoria Adams – Posh Spice (now Beckham, and undisputed queen of Footballers' Wives)

Geri Halliwell – Ginger Spice
Mel B – Scary Spice
Mel C – Sporty Spice
Emma Bunton – Baby Spice.

Maria Callas

"When my enemies stop hissing, I shall know I'm slipping."

Probably the best known opera singer of recent years, Maria Callas was renowned not only for her astounding voice, but also her dramatic and glamorous image, and her long-running affair with Aristotle Onassis. This lasted for 9 years, until he left her for Jackie Kennedy – which devastated Callas, and she went into a decline which lasted until her death in 1977, saying that 'First I lost my voice, then I lost my figure and then I lost Onassis'. Many years after her death, Franco Zeffirelli made a film about Callas claiming she had been poisoned by her pianist, Vasso Devetzi, so that she could inherit Callas's fortune, but this has never been substantiated.

Operatic Heroines

Carmen
Lucia di Lammermoor
Aida
Salome
Madame Butterfly

ELLA FITZGERALD. Dubbed 'The First lady of Song', 'The High Priestess of Song', 'mama Jazz', she won 13 Grammy Awards, and sold over 40 million albums in her lifetime.

"Music comes out of her. When she walks down the street, she leaves notes." Jimmy Rowles

KYLIE MINOGUE first became known as an actress for her role as Charlene in *Neighbours*, and the character's teen wedding to boyfriend Scott was one of the highlights of television in the late 1980's, attracting a record audience. She went on to become one of the top-selling artists of the hugely successful Stock, Aitken and Waterman stable, and after a downturn in her popularity, re-established herself as a major artist and a huge gay icon. At time of writing she is in the process of recovering from breast cancer, and her grace and dignity throughout her illness have been inspirational to many.

EARTHA KITT was born to an African American/Cherokee mother and a Caucasian father, at a time when mixed race marriages were still illegal in the US. A doyenne of the cabaret scene, she still performs regularly at Manhattan nightspots in her late 70s.

ISADORA DUNCAN is now remembered more for the manner of her death (she was strangled by her silk scarf when it became tangled in the wheels of a Bugatti) than her achievements in life. But in her day she was feted by European society, adored by all whom she danced for, it seems, and mobbed when she appeared in Berlin, where she was called 'Holy Isadora'.

From the release of her first album in 1983, MADONNA has courted controversy, and caused uproars with her unique brand of brash sexuality and lavish shows that frequently blend sexual and religious imagery in a way that has earned the wrath of the Catholic Church on more than one occasion. The original trendsetter, she's gone through what seems like hundreds of different images, from gold cone shaped bras and red lipstick, to Spanish senorita, earth mother, Marilyn-esque Hollywood bombshell, glam cowgirl...the list goes on. And her music has been as varied as her wardrobe – she constantly reinvents herself, which is one of the reasons she has been at the top of the business for so long. Another must be sheer, gritty tenacity, and a real talent not just for performance, but for the nuts and bolts of the business. Something of a poster girl for sexual liberation, she is a fiercely strong character who,whether or not you like her music, demands admiration.

ALISON KRAUSS, the country and bluegrass performer, has won 20 Grammy awards, more than any other female artist.

Following her, with 17 Grammys, is ARETHA FRANKLIN – the "Queen of Soul", who is regarded by many as one of the best vocal talents ever. She was the first woman to be inducted into the Rock and Roll Hall of Fame, and her voice was declared a natural resource by her home state of Michigan.

~

Female Winners of Grammy Album of the Year

Norah Jones
Alison Kraus
Emmy Lou Harris
Gilliam Welch
Lauryn Hill
Celine Dion
Alanis Morisette
Whitney Houston
Natalie Cole
Bonnie Raitt
Yoko Ono
Carole King
Stevie Nicks
Christine Buckingham
Barbra Streisand
Judy Garland

~

DAME JULIE ANDREWS, aka Mary Poppins and Maria von Trapp, embodies wholesome musical theatre, with her technically perfect, wide-ranging singing voice and extremely clean looking face.

MARLENE DIETRICH, she of the mysteriously arched eyebrows and smoky cabaret performance, starred in the first ever European talking film, *The Blue Angel*.

BESSIE SMITH, 1920s blues singer, was the highest paid black singer of her day, touring theatres and nightclubs. Her influence on female artists lived on after her death in a car accident, in artists such as Billie Holiday, Norah Jones and Janis Joplin.

Like Bessie, **BILLIE HOLIDAY** in turn influenced singers who came after her. One of the first black singers to perform alongside white musicians, she was one of the great jazz singers of all time.

Unlike JANIS JOPLIN, whose performances were dirty, and voice raw and unpolished, but immensely powerful and passionate. It's impossible to convey what was special about her as a performer in words – you just have to listen to her sing and take in the rasping, emotive, bourbon drenched quality of her. Her career was all too short – only three of her albums were released during her lifetime, with the majority coming posthumously, after her death from an accidental drug overdose at 27. But during her lifetime she had a huge impact – her big personality, her raucous laugh and sense of humour, her talent as a lyricist, her in-your-face, hippyish dress sense – all combined to make her one of the most memorable performers of her generation.

"When I'm there, I'm not here. I can't talk about my singing; I'm inside it. How can you describe something you're inside of?"

Crime and Punishment

~

ANNE BONNY and MARY READ – were pirates in the late
17th century, who terrorised the seas.

Anne was the illegitimate child of an Irish lawyer and one of
his maids. She disguised herself as a man in order to join the
crew of 'Calico' Jack Rackham (superstitious sailors
believed women on board a ship brought bad luck). When
the ship was attacked in 1720 most of the rest of the crew
were too drunk to defend it, and Anne and Mary warded off
the attack for a time. All the men were sentenced to death,
and Anne shouted to her lover "Had you fought like a man,
you need not have been hanged like a dog!"

BONNIE PARKER

You've read the story of Jesse James
Of how he lived and died,
If you're still in need for something to read
Here's the story of Bonnie and Clyde.

Bonnie Parker's reputation is bigger and badder than the
reality. It's possible, of course, that this is just the effect of

viewing her life from the ever more violent 21st century. The image of Bonnie as a ruthless, bloodthirsty killer is one that seems to have been created in popular imagination. When compiling the list of heroines for this book, Bonnie was put forward by various people. Why? She didn't do anything selfless, or creative, or inspiring. She wasn't beautiful particularly – though the photos she and Clyde Barrow took so many of show a certain sassy style. It's hard to find much information about her as a person that doesn't relate to her relationship with Clyde. But it's this relationship that seems to capture people's imagination. Love at first sight. Two lovers on the run – 'Romeo and Juliet in a Getaway Car' as they have been called.

Bonnie and Clyde and The Barrow Gang, as they and their cronies were known, committed a string of small hold-ups and robberies, and at least eleven people were killed by the group during their 2 years as fugitives. Bonnie herself never killed anyone, by all accounts, and it appears as if Clyde tried to keep her from being too involved in the crimes. They didn't always kill those who crossed their path – twice they kidnapped police officers who evidently expected to be murdered, only to leave them unharmed. They stole a series of cars, including one from an undertaker, in which they travelled around Texas and the surrounding states. The angry man chose to pursue them in a neighbour's car, a decision that led to his being tricked by the Barrow Gang, and squeezed into the back seat along with the robbers. They later treated him to hamburgers and left him with money to get home, before driving off in his car.

Bonnie and Clyde were doomed long before they died. Their

families are said to have arranged their burials before their deaths. Bonnie had no illusions about where they were headed – her poem, The Ballad of Bonnie and Clyde ends with the lines:

Someday they'll go down together
And they'll bury them side by side
To few it'll be grief, to the law a relief
But it's death for Bonnie and Clyde.

LUCREZIA BORGIA

The Borgias were a powerful family – the Corleones of 15th century Italy. Scandal and rumours of incestuous orgies abound, including a suggestion that Lucrezia's son, Giovanni, was fathered by either her father or her brother.

Lucrezia increased her family's power through a total of three clever marriages – she had been engaged twice by the time she was eleven, but both of these proposed unions were called off by her father. Her first wedding was conspicuously opulent, with a huge banquet and the bride attended by 500 ladies. The marriage was annulled on the grounds of non-consummation when her father's political leanings changed and her hapless husband was no longer useful to the Borgias. He at least survived his involvement with the family – no such luck for a chamberlain named Perrotto, who, after impregnating Lucrezia apparently 'fell into the Tiber against his will', nor her second husband, who was suffocated by her brother's servants.

She was rumoured to own a hollow ring, which she used to poison the drinks of those who had fallen out of favour.

~

Anti-Heroines

Lady Macbeth – Macbeth
Becky Sharp – Vanity Fair
Cruella de Ville – 101 Dalmations
Scarlett O'Hara – Gone With the Wind
The White Witch – Chronicles of Narnia
The Marquise de Merteuil – Les Liaisons Dangereuses
The Wicked Witch of the West – The Wizard of Oz
La Femme Nikita

~

CHING SHIH was a Chinese pirate who is said to have commanded around 1,500 ships, and has been called the 'best' pirate ever.

ELIZABETH BATHER was the first woman chief inspector in the Metropolitan Police, appointed in 1945.

MARY CARLETON – listed in the *Dictionary of National Biography* simply as 'impostor', she worked her way through various identities in her life of crime. She was married at least twice, and was indicted for bigamy on one occasion. She returned to Britain after a stay on the continent with a new identity, that of Maria de Wolway, a German noblewoman fleeing an unwanted marriage. As Maria she made a good marriage to a lawyer's clerk, but was unmasked as an impostor and thrown into jail not long afterwards. She was acquitted, in 1663.

She continued to dupe unwitting men, creating new identities complete with supporting documents as and when necessary, and was eventually hanged for her crimes.

PHOOLAN DEVI, otherwise known as India's Bandit Queen, was a modern day, female Robin Hood to poverty-stricken rural villagers. Married to a violent man at a young age, she left her husband only to be kidnapped by bandits. She became part of the gang of outlaws, eventually leading her own group of men, and her supporters claim she gave the spoils of her violent robberies to the poor. In a strange turnaround, she was elected as an MP in August 1996, where she served for five years, until she was murdered by unknown assailants.

GRACE O'MALLEY led a band of 16th century pirates and fought against English encroachment on Ireland. Her efforts culminated in a meeting with Elizabeth I, where Grace appeared before The Virgin Queen to ask for her a pardon for her sons, which Elizabeth granted.

HELL-CAT MAGGIE, member of the Dead Rabbit Gang in 19th Century New York, whose beauty was sharpened by her teeth, which she filed to points, and SADIE THE GOAT, who during the same period, head-butted her victims into submission.

~

Fictional Female Crime-fighters

Nancy Drew
Miss Marple
Jessica Fletcher
Kay Scarpetta

V.I. Warshawski
Charlie's Angels
Buffy the Vampire Slayer
George – The Famous Five

～

P.D. JAMES'S HEROINES

MADAME MARIE CURIE, *1867–1934. Polish-born French physicist who, with her husband, was awarded the Nobel prize for physics in 1903 for their work on radio therapy and, after her husband's death, the Nobel prize for chemistry in 1911.*

JANE AUSTEN, *1775–1817. She became one of England's major novelists despite the social and domestic demands imposed by her time and status.*

ELIZABETH FRY, *1780–1845. English Quaker who alleviated the appalling conditions of women in prison, among other charitable work.*

ROSAMUND FRANKLIN, *1920-58. English X-ray crystallographer whose work was of great value in the discovery of DNA but who died before she could receive full recognition.*

DAME CICELY SAUNDERS, *1918–2005. English founder of the modern hospice movement, which has developed into such an important part of palliative care.*

BELLE STARR THE BANDIT QUEEN was an outlaw known to some as the Petticoat Terror of the Plains. The subject of a multitude of rumours and tall tales, she was said to be the female Jesse James, and was a notorious robber and bootlegger. The epitaph on her grave, carved next to an image of a bell, a horse and a star, read:

Shed not for her the bitter tear,
Nor give the heart to vain regret;
'Tis but the casket that lies here,
The gem that filled it sparkles yet.

General Fabulousness

~

'Faaaabulous' seems to be something of a catchword for SHARON OSBOURNE. Already an important music manager, she shot to mass fame with *The Osbournes*, a docu-soap following the lives of herself, her husband Ozzy (infamous front-man of heavy metal band Black Sabbath), their three children, various animals and employees. Its appeal lay partly in Sharon's outspoken attitude, and her appearances on *The X Factor* have hit the headlines on several occasions because of her forthright opinions and penchant for swearing and throwing glasses of water over her fellow judges when riled. In the male dominated, hard-living, gruelling world of the music industry she has not only reached the top, but clung on to her position in deeply adverse circumstances. When she was diagnosed with cancer of the colon partway through the filming of the second season of *The Osbournes*, instead of cancelling, she allowed cameras to film her treatment and convalescence, with the aim of raising public awareness of an illness about which she felt there was too much embarrassment. Since then she has started The Sharon Osbourne Colon Cancer Program to continue with this aim and raise much needed funds, not only to go towards research, but to help less well-off patients cope with the effects of the disease and its treatment. And boy, can she shop...

"The virgin Mary speaks to me. She says, 'You must go to Tiffany. And on the way, stop at Cartier."

TRINNY AND SUSANNAH

'I'd rather eat my own hair than shop with these two again.' – Jeremy Clarkson

"Brillo-Pad hair", "Hair like a poodle", "Looked like Sly Stallone's mum", "She looked like the grim reaper", "Big Foot in men's clothes". These are just some of the insults that have been levelled at women taking part in Trinny and Sus's makeovers. They can just about get away with being such utter cows to people a lot of the time, ripping their victims' confidence and their wardrobe, quite literally, to shreds, before they build it back up with warmth and genuine empathy.

~

Most Fabulously Named Women

Ines de la Fressange
Gigi Levangie
Peaches Honeyblossom Michelle Charlotte Angel Vanessa Geldof
Heavenly Hiraani Tiger Lily Hutchence
Fifi Trixiebelle Geldof
Pixie Frou-Frou Geldof

Coco Chanel
Zsa Zsa Gabor
Eglantine Jebb
Endellion Lycett Green
Penelope Pitstop
Pearl Pureheart
Zelda Fitzgerald
Amandine Malkovich
Florence Nightingale
Parthenope Nightingale

DAISY ASHFORD

The author of the Victorian tale of love and marriage *The Young Visiters*, Daisy Ashford outclassed today's precocious child stars by writing this when she was just nine. She wrote nothing as an adult, and seems to exemplify the saying that everyone has one book in them – this is an extract from hers.

The Proposal:

Ethel he murmured in a trembly voice.

Oh what is it said Ethel hastily sitting up.

Words fail me ejaculated Bernard horsly my passion for you is intense he added fervently. It has grown day and night since I first beheld you.

Oh said Ethel in supprise I am not prepared for this and she lent back against the trunk of the tree.

Bernard placed one arm tightly round her. When will you marry me Ethel he uttered you must be my wife it has come to that I love you so intently that if you say no I shall perforce dash my body to the brink of yon muddy river he panted wildly.

Oh dont do that implored Ethel breathing rarther hard.

BIDDY BAXTER MBE produced *Blue Peter* from 1962–1965, and was the inventor of the legendary and much sought-after *Blue Peter* badge, which is awarded to winners of competitions and allows the bearer free entry into various attractions and events. Many of the traditions instigated by her and her team still run today, almost 50 years since it was first broadcast, such as the keeping of *Blue Peter* pets, annual charity appeals, 'Summer Expeditions'. The famous 'Makes' such as advent crowns, pet birthday cakes and handy jewellery organisers ('a perfect gift for Mother'...) always made use of copious amounts of double-sided sticky tape and the insides of loo-rolls, and there was always a 'Here's One I made Earlier'. The show goes out live, which has led to various mishaps over the years, such as defecating and escaping elephants and an out-of-control Girl Guide's bonfire.

VALERIE SINGLETON was quintessential seventies *Blue Peter*, remembered by Biddy Baxter for her unflappable nature. "If the studio roof collapsed in the middle of a live programme, Valerie would have stepped out of the rubble and said, 'And now for something quite different', without faltering."

Biddy Baxter is remembered fondly by many members of her team over the years for the sound of her ultra-high stiletto heels clipping down the stairs from control room to studio dozens of times per rehearsal, to give notes or makes comments.

~

Superheroines

Batgirl
The Bionic Woman
Catwoman
Elastigirl
Wonder Woman

~

Mabel Stark – The Tiger Queen

Dressed in flamboyant white leather bodysuits and knee-length boots, Mabel Stark was the World's Greatest Tiger Trainer, and one of the only female ones. Her date of birth is unclear (as are various details of her life – she gave herself a new name at least twice), as she changed her age to suit herself as she got older, but she was born some time in the late 19th century.

So how did a farmer's daughter from Kentucky, who started her working life as a nurse, become a tiger trainer, travelling across America with some of the country's greatest circuses? Nursing didn't last long – after less than a year Mabel had left – not quite run away with the circus, but become a cooch dancer (a form of burlesque). From this she progressed first to horseback rider and then to become the performing goat trainer – not the most inspiring or glamorous of circus job descriptions, but one that put her in a position to move further towards her goal of becoming Al G Barnes' tiger trainer (replacing Marguerite Kaupt, who had been killed by one of her charges). She achieved this by marrying the head cat trainer – her second husband (out of an eventual six).

Stark trained her cats with methods learnt from Roth – methods that were way ahead of their time. He had developed a system called 'gentling' which involved training the animals using what, in these post-Skinner and Pavlov days we might call positive reinforcement, giving them meat when they did what was asked of them, but which in 1912 was previously unheard of. Until then training had simply involved beating the animals until they obeyed – which might account for the high level of maulings suffered by tiger trainers.

As well as working almost exclusively with tigers (which are much harder to train and more dangerous than lions), constantly pushing the boundaries of her act to ten and then twelve tiger displays, which were bigger than had ever been performed before, Mabel developed the world's first tiger wrestling act with her tiger Rajah. The details of how she achieved this seemingly impossibly dangerous display (so much so that on many occasions members of the audience would leap out of their seats to try and get into the steel cage to save her) and explain why she only wore white bodysuits – it was to conceal the fact that the wrestling was in fact, frottage.

Mabel worked with tigers into her 80s, undeterred by multiple divorces, a fall from grace and subsequent sacking as a result of her marriage to an embezzling circus accountant, and a serious mauling by hungry tigers which she only just survived. She committed suicide in 1968.

Circus strongwoman KATIE SANDWINA met her husband during one of her wrestling challenges. He later became part of her act – she would lift the 165 pound man over her head with one arm.

DITA VON TEESE, burlesque artist extraordinaire, poses in

opulent, 1940s style, fishnet-clad legs sticking up out of claw-foot baths, riding diamante encrusted carousel horses, or dancing in an oversized martini glass. A modern day Vargas girl, she is famous for her 16 inch waist, her vampish yet tasteful image and her controversial rock-star husband Marilyn Manson.

"She has the style of a bird of paradise"
Christian Louboutin

IMMODESTY BLAIZE performs her burlesque act around the world, kicking up her heels on the back of a painted rocking horse or an oversized model of an old-fashioned telephone, or twirling silk parasols, resplendent in suspenders and nipple tassles. She sometimes uses a small terrier to collect her frilled and feathered stockings after her performance, and has not diamonds, but Swarovski crystals on the soles of her shoes, and can allegedly crack a pistachio between her thighs. Swoon.

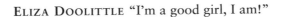

IMMODESTY BLAIZE'S HEROINES

Modesty Blaise
Ava Gardner
Josephine Baker
Aung San Suu Kyi
Lydia Thompson
Jessica Rabbit
Madonna

ELIZA DOOLITTLE "I'm a good girl, I am!"

NELL GIFFORD runs Gifford's Circus, an old-fashioned, magical, travelling extravaganza, which makes you yearn for an ideal childhood, with its dancing horses, acrobatics, star-painted drapes and upside-down tap dancing. Ringmaster of her troupe, the fishnet-stockinged Nell is creating something wonderful in the English countryside.

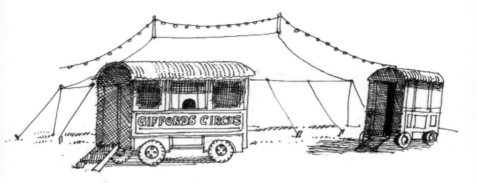

TARA PALMER-TOMKINSON, presenter of ITV2's coverage of *I'm a Celebrity Get Me Out of Here!*, the jungle-based reality TV show, co-hosts the programme with her signature witty and slightly crazed style. Her enthusiasm, her unpredictable nature and her refusal to take herself too seriously have helped make her Britain's favourite posh girl pin-up.

TARA PALMER-TOMKINSON'S HEROINES

Audrey Hepburn
Jessica Rabbit
Vivienne Westwood

THE MITFORD SISTERS – NANCY, PAMELA, DIANA, UNITY, JESSICA ('DECCA') and DEBO, were the darlings of 1930s society. Beautiful, aristocratic and eccentric, they continue to epitomise the between the war years.

Nancy, the eldest of the 6 sisters, is justifiably loved and famous today because of her novels which present a fictionalised version of the family's unconventional childhood. *The Pursuit of Love* and *Love in a Cold Climate* are wonderful, funny, romantic books which are loved by everyone I have spoken to who has read them. They capture your heart in a way few books do. She was also a notable biographer, and writer on class issues – her book *Noblesse Oblige* provided a guide to Upper Class English behaviour and terminology.

Jessica was also a writer, chronicled the sisters' childhoods in her memoir *Hons and Rebels*, and wrote an important treatise on the funeral industry in *The American Way of Death*. She was an ardent Communist, which resulted in a long running feud with her sisters Unity and Diana.

Diana Mitford is now notorious for her friendship with Adolf Hitler, but was also, as the wife of Bryan Guinness, one of the most celebrated hostesses and beauties of London. She later married the fascist Oswald Mosley, whose mistress she had been, and the couple were imprisoned at Holloway for much of World War II.

Unity's fascist sympathies were so strong (she is generally acknowledged to have been in love with Hitler) that her distress when war broke out was such that she shot herself in the head in a failed suicide attempt. Though she did not die immediately, complications from the injuries caused her eventual death.

Pamela Mitford was the least rebellious of the girls, who married the *News of the World* heir Derek Jackson, and led a relatively conventional life.

The only surviving Mitford sister today is Debo, Dowager Duchess of Devonshire. Her great achievement has been the restoration and revitalisation of Chatsworth House, one of the country's finest seats, and its transformation into a highly successful business and local employer.

Collectively the Mitford sisters perhaps appear to be more than the sum of their parts, and today one can overlook the political views that might otherwise appear distasteful. Their passion and glamour seems to transcend them – they threw themselves into life, in a variety of ways – they loved, and danced the night away, "in all the diamonds I could lay my hands on," as Diana once said.

JESSICA RABBIT, the ultimate cartoon pin-up from *Who Framed Roger Rabbit*, is apparently something of a collage of bombshells, with body parts inspired by Marilyn Monroe (torso and bottom), Veronica Lake (hair style), Marlene Dietrich (eyes), Betty Grable (legs) and Jayne Mansfield (breasts).

"I'm not bad, I'm just drawn that way."

ANNIE OAKLEY was born in a log cabin in Ohio and went on to star in Buffalo Bill's Wild West Show as a legendary sharp-shooter. The inspiration for the musical *Annie Get Your Gun*, she could shoot a coin thrown into the air at 90

feet, shoot the ash from a cigarette held in the mouth of her partner, Frank Butler, and shoot holes in a playing card as it fluttered to the floor.

MAE WEST was perhaps destined for an unusual life; her father was a prize-fighter, policeman and later private detective, and her mother was a corset model. A vaudeville performer from the age of 5, she later spent 8 days in jail on charges of public obscenity, where she apparently charmed the warder into allowing her to wear non-regulation silk knickers. She later played opposite Cary Grant and other leading men of the day, and is perhaps best known for the witty double entendres with which she peppered her sentences.

'I consider sex to be a misdemeanour – the more I miss, de meaner I get'.

~

KATHY LETTE'S HEROINES

Heroines. I am a heroine addict. Self confessed. And I don't want to be cured. I admire so many women. But my favourite addictions are Becky Sharp, Jane Austen, Mae West, Mary Woolstonecraft, Germaine Greer and Simone de Beauvoir.

BECKY SHARP
With tongue in chic and lashings of chutzpuh, Becky was the Madonna of her day, flaunting tradition and challenging hypocritical sexual mores. Okay, she had a few minor faults – snobbery and sexual kleptomania (Becky climbed the social ladder – lad by lad); husband-hunting (she wasn't interested in Mr Right, but Lord, Sir, Marquis Right at the very least)...But we're talking 1810. With no vote, no union, no fixed wage, no welfare, no contraception...what options were available to women? Apart from factory work, governessing or domestic service, it was prostitution or marriage. (Often a tautology in those days.)

JANE AUSTEN'S acerbic satirical style is more controlled than a pair of Liz Taylor's panty hose. A barbed commentator on the battle between the sexes, Austen realised that, as a woman, poetic justice was the only justice in the world –

and set about impaling misogynistic enemies on the end of her pen.

As British women still don't enjoy equal pay (we're getting around 75 pence in the pound) and are still getting concussion from hitting our heads on the glass ceiling (as well as being expected to Windex it while we're up there), any woman who calls herself a post feminist, has kept her wonder bra but burnt her brains. To cure this ideological rot, The Second Sex *(Simone de Beauvoir),* The Female Eunuch *(Germaine Greer), and* The Rights of Woman *(Mary Woolstonecraft) should be fed intravenously to every young woman the world over as an antidote to men who are bent on disproving the theory of evolution by evolving INTO apes.*

MAE WEST

had a black belt in the art of tongue-fu. As well as being famous for breasts which arrived five minutes before she did, her wit should have been registered at Police Headquarters as a lethal weapon. By the time she died in 1980, her minestrone mix of talent had made her a successful comedian, singer, dancer, playwright, director, actress, scriptwriter, producer, Sex Goddess and novelist.

Yet despite her status as a cultural "come up and see me sometime" icon, she remained down to earth – a self made woman, who didn't worship her creator.

∼

CALAMITY JANE was an expert and fearless rider from a young age, and a sharp-shooter in Buffalo Bill's Wild West

Show. Before this, she worked as a scout for General Custer, dressed as a man, and as an express rider carrying the mail over rough trails, through dangerous terrain filled with highwaymen. She said of this time:

'I was molested very little, for the toll gatherers looked on me as being a good fellow, and they knew that I never missed my mark.'

'STAGECOACH MARY' FIELDS was a 6 foot tall, 200 pound former slave who had a standing bet that she could knock any man out cold with a single punch. Self-appointed protector of the nuns at the Ursuline convent where she worked – that is, until she was fired by the bishop following a shoot-out where a number of his shirts were torn through by Mary's bullets. She got her name from the mail route she ran after this, delivering mail to remote cabins in all weather.

TALLULAH BANKHEAD was wild and witty and beautiful – a fellow member of the Algonquin Round Table admitted that "she was so pretty that we thought she must be stupid", a mistake that many others were to make during her lifetime. Renowned for her outrageous behaviour and massive consumption of cigarettes, drugs and alcohol as well as her looks, she was investigated by MI5 for allegedly seducing schoolboys at Eton, and never achieved the acclaim as an actress that she so desperately wanted. She died gasping for "*Codeine...bourbon.*"

The ultimate flapper, epitome of the Jazz Age, and darling of New York society, ZELDA FITZGERALD inspired many of her husband F. Scott Fitzgerald's female characters. Living out of suitcases in luxurious hotels and villas, the Fitzgeralds travelled the world, spending money like water, and hosting notoriously debauched parties. At one such event, Zelda, ever jealous of other women, became so enraged by a conversation between Scott and Isadora Duncan that she pretended to leap from a cliff. Their relationship was passionate and fiery, and they argued frequently. It has been said that their neighbours in the French Riviera, where they used to summer, could always tell when they had been rowing, because Zelda's trunks would be lying, half-packed, in the street come morning, having been abandoned when Scott eventually persuaded her back inside. Despite the volatile nature of their marriage, Scott and Zelda remained deeply entangled even after they had separated and throughout his alcoholism and her years in mental hospitals. She died in a fire in hospital.

"I don't want to live. I want to love first, and live incidentally."

Pilgrims and Pioneers

MARGARET MEE was a botanical artist who travelled through the Amazonian rainforests in pursuit of rare flowers, with her watercolours and straw hat and pistol, in a small boat with a local guide. Some of her early illustrations are especially important as they document areas which have

now all but disappeared, and in 1971 she discovered an area containing many new species, which have never been found before or since, and of which her paintings are the only known record.

FREYA STARK

One of the great women travellers and mountaineers, Freya Stark spent years exploring the world alone, venturing into places most travellers of her age would never dream of going with an experienced guide and armed guard, let alone as a single woman. She trekked through the infamous Valley of the Assassins. She was thrown into military prison, discovered hidden routes of the incense trade, and lived with Bedouins in their desert camps.

"To awaken quite alone in a strange town is one of the pleasantest sensations in the world."

ELLEN MACARTHUR sailed 27,000 miles around the world single-handed, breaking the record for a solo round the

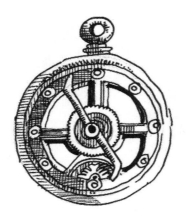

world trip aged just 28, despite nearly colliding with a whale, and contending with serious burn injuries, icebergs, and gale force winds. Only the second person ever to complete such a journey in the type of boat she used, Ellen bought her first boat by saving her school dinner money, and sailed round Britain alone when she was 18. She became Britain's youngest Dame in 2005.

Despite her adventures and trials along the yellow brick road, at the end of *The Wizard of Oz* it turns out that all DOROTHY has to do to return home to Kansas is click her heels together. If only it were that simple for some of the other travellers here...

LADY MARY WORTLEY MONTAGU

Writer and traveller, she was responsible for introducing the smallpox vaccination to the West after discovering that inoculation was common practice in Turkish folk medicine, travelling to hospitals and sick beds extolling the virtues of the vaccination, taking her young daughter with her as living proof of its efficacy.

Pioneering war reporter and journalist MARTHA GELLHORN had a career that spanned over 60 years, during which time she covered nearly every major conflict that took place. She was the first journalist to report from Dachau concentration camp following its liberation, and later wrote about the Vietnam war, the Arab-Israeli Six -Day War, and the US invasion of Panama (by which time she was 81).

ANN DANIELS, the first British female Polar guide, was part of the first all-female team to conquer both the North and South poles, along with **CAROLINE HAMILTON** and **POM OLIVER**, a trip which took them 81 days.

MARY KINGSLEY undertook expeditions to West Africa in the late 19th century, returning to England with a huge collection of plants, shells, reptiles and fish, including three new species which were named after her.

She spoke out against the attempts of the missionaries to 'Europeanize Africans', and appealed for a greater understanding of Africa and its unique culture and society.

Her description of falling into a spiked game pit is typically bracing: "It is at these times you realise the blessing of a good thick skirt," and she recounts her fights with hippopotami and crocodiles in a singularly unimpressed tone.

ELIZA BRADLEY wrote a book entitled "*An Authentic Narrative of the Shipwreck and Sufferings of Mrs Eliza Bradley, The Wife of Capt. James Bradley, of Liverpool, Commander of the Ship Sally, which was wrecked on the Coast of Barbary, in June, 1818. The crew and passengers of the above Ship fell into the hands of the Arabs a few days after their Shipwreck.*"

"*After enduring incredible Hardships during Six Months Captivity (Five of which she was separated from her Husband, and every other Civilized Being) she was fortunately Redeemed out of the Hands of the Unmerciful Barbarians, by Mr Willshire, the British Consul, Resident at Mogadore. Written by Herself.*"

GERTRUDE BELL was a traveller and explorer who went further than any other lone woman of her time into Arabia. She had been fascinated by the country since travelling to Jerusalem to learn Arabic, and was later proclaimed an honorary man by the Arabs, for whose independence she campaigned for many years. Described by sheik Fahad Bey as only a woman 'but a mighty and valiant one', she documented her travels, undertaking archaeological projects and excavations and translating Persian poetry (after teaching herself the language). With the outbreak of World War I her knowledge of the country became invaluable to the British Forces, and she was employed as their only female political officer, and later helped with the delineation of the borders of the new country of Iraq. She killed herself with a bottle of sleeping pills and was buried in Baghdad with full military honours.

ISABELLE EBERHARDT was another traveller who became entranced by the lure of Arabia, and also taught herself the language and converted to Islam. Frequently dressed as a man, she lived a bohemian life, smoking hashish and taking lovers as it suited her, while also receiving religious instruction, and scandalising the French colonists with her antics. An assassination attempt followed in 1901, and her assailant claimed he had been ordered by Allah to kill her. The ensuing trial only served to increase her notoriety, and she was ordered to leave Africa. She returned after marrying her Arab lover, and died in a flash flood in the Sahara.

DAISY BATES emigrated to Australia to live among the aborigines in 1899, where she spent over 30 years documenting the Aborigines' birth, burial and circumcision rituals, filing detailed maps and reports and being named as an honorary man by the tribespeople. She was initiated into the 'freedom of all the totems', a complex ceremony that made her a friend of all the Aboriginal tribes, and did so wearing 'a sober European coat and skirt, a sailor hat with a veil, and neat, high-heeled shoes'. She allegedly learnt over one hundred tribal languages, and completed a 3,000 mile cattle drive across West Australia

MARIANNE NORTH travelled all over the world painting its most beautiful and exotic flowers. From Yosemite to Tenerife, Japan to Singapore, she watercoloured her way through inhospitable terrain on dug-out canoes and pony

carts, leaving behind her a gallery of hundreds of paintings of flowers and plants.

SUSAN TRAVERS was the only woman to have joined the French Foreign Legion, after becoming a member of the French Red Cross when the Second World War broke out. She was awarded the *Croix de Guerre* and the *Ordre du Corps d'Arme* for her part in the *Battle of Bir Hakeim*, and later, the *Médaille Militaire* and the *Légion d'Honneur*.

ROSAMUND FRANKLIN has been called the 'unsung hero of the search for the structure of DNA' who conducted ground-breaking work into viruses. As a result of her X-ray crystallography work on DNA, she proposed the helical structure, and gave a lecture on it. This was attended by, among others, Watson & Crick, who later published a paper based on her theories just before Franklin was able to do so herself, and broke a 'gentleman's' agreement they had made with her (by working on DNA when they had claimed not to be).

DOROTHY HODGKIN, winner of the Nobel Prize for Chemistry, determined the structure of penicillin, vitamin B12  and insulin, which meant that the drugs could be synthesized, making treatment possible for thousands more people. She used the prize money she was awarded to set up a scholarship, working towards peace and famine relief.

She is the only British female scientist to have been awarded the Nobel Prize.

RACHEL CARSON is often credited with launching the environmental movement globally with the publication of her 1962 book *The Silent Spring*, which criticized industrial society and explained the far-reaching negative effects of the use of pesticides. It had a huge effect, especially in Carson's native America, where the pesticide policy was reversed as a result of her writings. There was also a major counter-attack to the book, and Carson was derided as a 'hysterical woman', called unprofessional, 'a mere bird-watcher' and denounced as a Communist.

~

Winners of the Nobel Prize for Medicine

Gerty Cori – 1947
Rosalyn Yallow – 1977
Barbara McClintock – 1983
Rita Levi-Montalcini – 1986
Gertrude B. Elion – 1988
Christiane Nusslein-Volhard – 1995
Linda B. Buck – 2004

~

No woman has been awarded the Nobel Prize for Economics.

As the first female Italian physician, MARIA MONTESSORI graduated from the University of Rome in 1894. After achieving her medical status, she began working with so called 'idiot' children, many of whom had previously been thought to be uneducable, and had unprecedented success teaching them. Some of the children entered state examinations for 'normal' children. She began to open specialist schools, developing her theories and the now famous 'Montessori Method' along the way.

"Keep your face to the sunshine and you cannot see the shadow."
Helen Keller

When HELEN KELLER began writing about blindness in books and magazines, in the early part of the 20th century, the subject was still somewhat shrouded in mystery, as blindness was thought to be frequently caused by venereal disease. Left deaf-blind by an illness when a toddler, by the age of seven she had developed her own set of signs to communicate with her family, and later learnt to speak using the Tadoma method, which involves touching the lips and throats of people while they speak, and 'fingerspelling' letters on the palm of her hand. She later learnt five other languages in Braille. She became the first deaf-blind person to graduate from college aged 24, and began her work writing and campaigning, not just for causes related to her disability, but for pacifism, women's rights, and in support of birth control, the working classes and socialism. She was awarded the highest civilian honour in America in 1964, the Presidential Medal of Freedom, by President Johnson, among other awards and accolades. Helen Keller International, formed initially to help soldiers blinded during WWI, funds health and nutrition programs to help combat nutrition-based blindness, among other projects around the world.

"Helen Keller is fellow to Caesar, Alexander, Napolean, Homer, Shakespeare, and the rest of the immortals. She will be as famous a thousand years from now as she is today."
Mark Twain.

LAURA INGALLS WILDER, wrote the *Little House on the Prairie* series about her pioneering life growing up in a log cabin in Kansas, detailing the family's struggles to survive the harsh winters, terrifying incidents with 'injuns', butter churning and prairie fire.

"Then Pa gave her a little wooden man he had whittled out

of a stick, to be company for Charlotte. Ma gave her five little cakes, one for each year that Laura had lived with her and Pa. And Mary gave her a new dress for Charlotte. Mary had made the dress herself, when Laura thought she was sewing on her patchwork quilt..."
Little House in the Big Woods

Great Lovers

JANE EYRE, beloved of the glowering Mr Rochester, eventually gets her man at the end of the novel, blind and maimed from a terrible fire, after many interruptions from mad Creole wives in the attic, unexpected inheritances, and a narrow escape from marriage to the terminally turgid Revd. Rivers. The novel ends with the now immortal words "Reader, I married him."

WALLIS WARFIELD SIMPSON (WINDSOR)

"You can't abdicate and eat it"

The demonised Duchess, The Woman who Cost a Kingdom, The Lowest of the Low, The Woman I Love...

A society belle, Wallis Windsor was on her second marriage by the time she met Edward, Prince of Wales in 1931. Part of the smart and 'fast' set, she was the subject of much gossip, which only increased when Edward abdicated on 10 December 1936 in order to marry her and the couple moved to semi-exile in France.

Isolde and Tristan
Cleopatra and Antony
Juliet and Romeo
Scarlett O'Hara and Rhett Butler
Bonnie and Clyde
Priscilla and Elvis Presley
Elizabeth Taylor and Richard Burton
Zelda and Scott Fitzgerald
Minnie and Mickey Mouse

HÉLOÏSE

The French abbess is one of the original lovers. Niece of Canon Fulbert in 12th century France, who encouraged her to study (a rare thing for a woman to do at the time) Héloïse committed the sin of first falling desperately in love with her tutor, Abelard, and then having a child by him out of wedlock. The couple eventually married, in an attempt to appease Fulbert. But Héloïse was worried that the marriage went against the philosophical ideal that Abelard had pursued so single-mindedly until that point. It was also likely to limit his career in the church. So the marriage was kept secret, and afterwards Héloïse entered a convent.

Fulbert was apparently so enraged by what he viewed as an abandonment of his niece and ward, that he took revenge on Abelard, ordering a group of servants to break into Abelard's rooms one night and castrate him. Abelard became a monk, and wrote the *Historia Calamitatum* – or

'Story of my Misfortunes'. Years later Héloïse received a copy of this and wrote directly to Abelard. Her love for Abelard and bitterness at their situation are clear.

"While we enjoyed the pleasures of an uneasy love and abandoned ourselves to fornication (if I may use an uglier but more expressive word) we were spared God's severity. But when we amended our unlawful conduct by what was lawful, and atoned for the shame of fornication by an honourable marriage, then the Lord in his anger laid his hand heavily upon us, and would not permit a chaste union though he had long tolerated one which was unchaste. The punishment you suffered would have been proper vengeance for men caught in open adultery. But what others deserve for adultery came upon you through a marriage which you believed had made amends for all previous wrong doing; what adulterous women have brought upon their lovers, your own wife brought on you."

Heloise remained in the convent for the rest of her life. When Abelard died his body was entombed there, until she died twenty-two years later and joined him.

LADY ISABEL BURTON

One of the indomitable Victorian women explorers, she followed her husband, Richard Burton, around the world, and dedicated her life to supporting and loving him. They translated *The Arabian Nights* together, and she wrote about their passionate love affair in a memoir, *The Romance of Lady Isabel Burton*, from which this description of their first encounter comes.

"He looked at me as though he read me through and through in a moment, and started a little, I was completely magnetized, and when we had got a little distance away, I turned to my sister, and whispered to her, 'That man will marry me'."

ARTEMISIA OF CARIA was the wife of Mausolus, and was so devastated by his death that she is reputed to have drunk a solution containing his ashes daily during the two years that she survived him, pining all the while. She built the Mausoleum at Helicarnassus, one of the 7 Wonders of the World, in his memory.

Almost always pictured head to toe in bubblegum pink, BARBARA CARTLAND was probably the world's most prolific and popular romance novelist, selling over a billion books. She rated the longest entry in *Who's Who*, and the *Guinness Book of Records* named her the top selling author in the world. Rather daring in her youth, penning a risqué novel and even a banned play, she became far more conservative as she grew older. Her books (all 724 of them...) were famously so and as attitudes became more and more liberal, she was ridiculed by critics. Her heroines were chaste and her heroes powerful, moody and passionate, and titles such as *The Frightened Bride*, *The Duke and the Preacher's Daughter*, and *The Taming of Lady Lorinda* indicate that the scenarios changed little from story to story.

"His heart was frantically beating against Demelza's as he drew her close and still closer. Then there was the fragrance of honeysuckle and the haunting mystery and inescapable wonder of love which was as free as the wind, as deep as the ocean and as high as the sky."

During World War Two, Barbara Cartland paid for 1,000 wedding dresses, which were then hired by the day to brides in need of a dress to marry in, for which generosity she received the Certificate of Merit.

Prior to her death, she wrote her own obituary, entitled *How I Wish to be Remembered*, and sent it to journalists tied up with a pink ribbon.

Perhaps best known for her two marriages to Richard Burton, ELIZABETH TAYLOR has had six other husbands in her life. An extremely beautiful child actress, making her screen debut when she was 9 years old, she played opposite Burton in a handful of films and their romance was one of the most public and captivating of its time.

Famous also for her love of jewels, Burton gave her various enormous 'baubles', including the Burton-Taylor diamond, a 69.42 carat rock that he described as 'having so many carats, it's almost a turnip'. She also started the Elizabeth Taylor AIDS Foundation, which has distributed millions of dollars to AIDS service organisations worldwide.

ZSA ZSA GABOR has tied the knot 9 times, with her unions lasting from just one day, to over 13 years, even finding a new husband in one of her divorce lawyers. She famously proclaimed that a girl must 'marry for love, and keep on marrying until she finds it'. It has been said that her many and lucrative divorce settlements made her the most expensive courtesan since Madame de Pompadour.

QUEEN SURIYOTHAI, in 16th century Siam, died on the back of a war elephant. Dressed as a man (as women were not allowed to enter battle) she followed her husband into battle, secretly, and when the King fell from his mount, she died of the wound from an arrow meant for him.

LADY JANE DIGBY – explorer, adventurer, and multiple marrier...married and divorced for the first time when only 17, her various bonds to a string of titled husbands made her Lady Ellenborough, Baroness Venningen, Countess Theotoky, and Mrs. Sheik Abdul Medjuel El Mezrub. Her affairs spawned 6 children, a duel, and at least one elopement. She also had affairs with such notable lovers as King Ludwig of Bavaria, and his son, King Otho of Greece, Honoré de Balzac, and the future Napoleon III. Despite having lots of children, she never seemed very fond of them, often leaving them with their fathers when she moved on to the next great love of her life, until she met her final husband, Medjuel, with whom she lived for almost thirty years, apparently blissfully happy, in Damascus and the desert, washing his feet and accompanying him into inter-tribal battles.

~

Fictional Floozies

Moll Flanders
Fanny Hill
Nana
Nancy Sykes

~

16th century Venetian courtesan VERONICA FRANCO followed her mother into her profession, which allowed her unusual freedom for the time. Writer of explicitly sexual poetry, she asserted her right to love whoever she chose, and had affairs with many of the prominent men in Venetian society as well as with the King of France. Her way of life and intelligence were clearly viewed as a threat, as in 1580 she was put on trial by the Inquisition and charged with using witchcraft to make men fall in love with her – a charge of which she was eventually acquitted.

NELL GWYNNE, orange seller at the Theatre Royal, actress, and Charles II's mistress was rumoured to have also been a pimp at the theatre, once broke up a fight between two men, one of whom had called her a whore, with the words "I *am* a whore. Find something else to fight about.*"*

Another famous courtesan, EMMA HAMILTON, started her career in a brothel, and was mistress to various aristocratic men of the late 17th century, before meeting Admiral Nelson in 1793, when he was gathering reinforcements against the French and she was living the high life in Italy as a friend of Queen Caroline of Naples. She was still married when she became Nelson's lover in 1799, and when he returned from war she nursed him (in her marital home) and apparently threw his 40th birthday party for him, inviting over 1,000 guests. Left fortunes by both her husband and her lover, they ran through her fingers quickly, and she was arrested for bankruptcy shortly before her death from alcoholism, penniless, in 1815.

Great Romantic Heroines

Anna Karenina
Scarlett O'Hara – Gone With the Wind
Catherine Moorland – Wuthering Heights
Jane Eyre
Lolita
Linda Kroesig – The Pursuit of Love
Lady Chatterley – Lady Chatterley's Lover
Madame Bovary
Bridget Jones

Elizabeth Bennett – Pride and Prejudice
Emma
Madame Butterfly
Violetta Valery – La Traviata
Rebecca
Guinevere
Lois Lane

~

MARIE DUPLESSIS was the French 19th century courtesan and mistress who became the inspiration for *Le Dame aux Camélias*, and in turn, the main character in *La Traviata* and various feature films including *Moulin Rouge*.

MARGARET FOUNTAINE

Author of *Love Among the Butterflies* this Victorian lepidopterist was an equally ardent collector of lovers, beginning  her amorous career with an imagined engagement to a chorister, and including a long liaison with her married Syrian interpreter/guide. She amassed a collection of over 20,000 butterflies. Fewer lovers, hopefully.

~

Madames

MADAME PAULINE – Santa Cruz saloon owner who was praised for her generosity to the poor.

HEIDI FLEISS – Her little black book threatened to scandalise half of Hollywood.

POLLY ADLER – "My girls gave a man his money's worth."

SYDNEY BIDDLE BARROWS – The Mayflower Madam, whose high class agency was renowned for how well its girls were treated.

~

Artists and Aesthetes

~

GRANDMA MOSES

"If I didn't start painting, I would have raised chickens."

Grandma Moses was a folk artist who began painting in her seventies because arthritis had put a stop to her embroidery. Her paintings were discovered in the late 1930s by an art dealer and quickly became extremely popular. One of her works which was bought for $110 in the forties was valued in 2004 at $60,000.

PEGGY GUGGENHEIM may have been the most influential patron of American art ever, collecting and supporting the work of artists such as Matisse,

Picasso, Braque and Klee, buying pieces from shows herself in order to encourage the artists. She showed unpopular and controversial artists, building up their reputations and followings. The Peggy Guggenheim Collection, in Venice, houses this important selection of 20th century European and American art. She is buried in the sculpture garden on the estate, next to her dogs.

BERTHE MORISOT, the Impressionist painter, was one of only two artists who exhibited in all of the Impressionist shows, and is considered to be one of the most important women artists of the 19th century, alongside MARY CASSATT.

~

EMMA BRIDGEWATER'S HEROINES

JOAN OF ARC, *because she was so brave and dashing, leading her soldiers into battle, also she always seemed to be given a rather groovy hairdo by illustrators.*

EMMYLOU HARRIS, *because she sings like an angel with a soaring smoky voice, and also because after several marriages she decided she was no good at that and went back home to live with her Mum. Sensible.*

ELIZABETH FRY, *because she did so much to improve society's attitude to prisons, for women in particular. Hers was the belief that prison could and should be an opportunity for education and redemption. We could do with sitting her down with the Home Secretary right now.*

ROSALIND *in* As You Like It, *because I love that cross-dressing thing. I admire women who find ways to escape and spend time with other versions of themselves.*

GEORGETTE HEYER, *for offering an escape hatch to an altogether cosier place; she made a world in her novels to which I retreat when I just can't face my own challenges and need a couple of hours off. With a tall dark handsome hellrake for company.*

ELIZABETH DAVID *because despite the energetic innovation and colourful tv exposure of her counterparts today, no one comes close to her for bone-hard, cool prose. I've never bought the idea that she writes porn...mystifying.*

JUNE CARTER *because she sang at The Opry, she danced,*

she toured with Elvis and Jerry-Lee (lucky, lucky her) and most of all because she loved her husband so sweetly. If not for her, no Johnny Cash.

TAD LUCAS, *a Rodeo Cowgirl born in Texas in 1902. I have chosen her as an archetype of the bold and competent ranching women who made America and who seem to me to embody many of the best things about the country. I know I ought to admire the women who toiled as missionaries, I do in many ways. But they always make me feel claustrophobic. I hope I would have made the grade as a 'Madonna of the Prairies'.*

FRIDA KAHLO was a Mexican painter who is easily recognisable in her self-portraits, which make up around a third of her body of work, because of her slightly exaggerated portrayal of her mono-brow and moustache. Her work is brightly coloured and stylized, and often reflects her physical suffering (as a result of childhood polio, recurrent miscarriages and severe injuries sustained in a bus accident). She is alleged to have had an affair with Trotsky, whom she protected during his appeal for asylum from the Soviet Union.

The sculptor BARBARA HEPWORTH is regarded as one of the most important 20th Century artists with her larger abstract forms which can be seen in sculpture parks and public spaces around Britain. She was a founder member of the St Ives Group of artists, her work was exhibited in numerous international exhibitions and bought by most major galleries around the world. She died in a fire at her St Ives studio in 1965.

Fellow sculptor DAME ELISABETH FRINK has focused her work on the male form, particularly male heads, creating strong, sometimes menacing bronze figures.

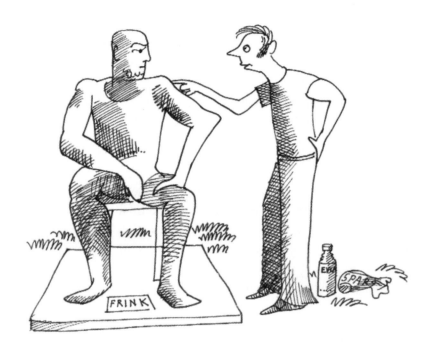

Four and More-Legged

LAIKA, THE DOG became the first living creature to orbit the earth, aboard the Soviet satellite, Sputnik 2, in 1957.

BARBARA WOODHOUSE, famous for her tweed skirts and her 'Walkies' as well as her ability to teach basic obedience skills in under 6 minutes, claimed to have a telepathic connection with the animals she trained. She held the world record for dog training, with over 17,000 of them passing through her doors during her career. She taught one of her own dogs to answer the telephone.

PULCINELLA was the pet cat of composer Scarlatti, whose journeys up and down the keyboard inspired *The Cat's Fugue*.

LUCINDA GREEN MBE, NÉE PRIOR-PALMER is World Champion Three-Day Eventer, has won the Badminton horse trials a record 6 times on 6 different horses, the only rider to have done so. She has also won the Collins trophy a record 7 times. Eventing is one of the few sports where men and women compete on equal terms, which makes her achievements all the more notable. Lady Sophy Topley describes a meeting with her.

"I have always thought modesty with achievement one of the most glamorous characteristics, and I remember Lucinda giving a marvellous example of this. She was competing in the One Day Event at Chatsworth during the 1980s. At this time she was a household name as World Champion and winner of Badminton a record six times. A number of people, including her, were staying at Chatsworth over the Horse trials weekend, some of them not involved in horses at all. At lunch Lucinda came in. She had done her dressage and show jumping and was due to ride cross country later in the afternoon – so one would have expected her to be preoccupied with the final discipline. However, she had taken the trouble to change out of her riding clothes into a smart skirt, and sat down between two unhorsey people and talked to them about topics which interested them. Not only did her interlocutors have no idea of her world wide fame, but they were even unaware she was competing that day. I call that very stylish". So do I.

ANNA SEWELL'S only publication was *Black Beauty*, which was originally intended for those who worked with horses, to encourage kindness and good treatment of their charges, but went on to become the sixth best-selling book in the English language.

Raymond Chandler read the first drafts of his mystery novels to TAKI, his 'feline secretary'.

~

Fictional Female Animals

Lassie
Elsa the Lioness – Born Free
Angelina Ballerina
Minnie Mouse
Nana – Peter Pan
Lady – Lady and the Tramp
Black Beauty
The Empress of Blandings – Blandings Castle
Miss Piggy
Charlotte – Charlotte's Web
Kanga – Winnie the Pooh

~

CATARINA was Edgar Allen Poe's cat, and the inspiration for his story *The Black Cat*.

~

Characters from Cats

Bombalurina
Cassandra
Grizabella
Lady Griddlebone
Jellylorum
Jemima
Jennyanydots
Rumpleteazer
Victoria

~

JILLY COOPER'S HEROINES

Being horse-mad, I've always loved the Pullein-Thompson sisters, Diana, Josephine and Christine, and their wonderful books about ponies and the children who ride them. They wrote wonderful English and embroidered their prose with quotations from poems, and many of the wonderful quotations I know today come from those books.

Other heroines are women who lessen the suffering of animals. Dorothy Brooke, who went to Egypt in the early twenties and was so horrified by the starving horses pulling impossible heavy weights in the streets and the stone quarries. On investigating further she discovered the horses had fought incredibly bravely to help us win the 1914–1918 war. Instead of returning home to a nice peaceful future in green fields they were sold to the Egyptians who would pay a lot of money for a working horse. Dorothy Brooke wrote a fierce letter to The Times *and raised enough money to build a hospital in Egypt. She rescued hundreds of horses and the hospital is still doing marvellous work today.*

I admire Brigitte Bardot because beauty seemed much less important to her than improving the lives of animals and she flew over to Scotland to speak at a court case and rescued some poor dog that was going to be put down for biting a postman.

I also hugely admire Lady Fretwell, a wonderful woman who headed a successful campaign to introduce Passport for Pets into this country, enabling people to take their animals abroad with them, and also rescue and bring home strays that were suffering horribly abroad.

Another heroine is Georgette Heyer, whose romantic and very funny historical novels taught me a huge amount of history and made my rather austere boarding school bearable, because I could constantly dream of getting off with one of her incredibly glamorous and aristocratic heroes.

I hugely admire the Queen because I think she's beautiful and funny and brave and incredibly hard-working and there is something so sweet and kind about her when you meet her. She immediately puts you at your ease. I think she hasn't put a foot wrong in eighty years.

One of the first inductees into the British Horse Society Equestrian Hall of Fame, SHEILA WILCOX was the first lady eventer to achieve international success, winning Badminton horse trials for three consecutive years between 1957 and 1959.

Chameleons and Butterflies

~

SARAH HOBSON travelled solo through Iran disguised as a boy in 1970, when she was 24, on a motorbike called Mephistopheles.

Various women throughout history have dressed as boys or men in order to take to the seas, such as MARY ANNE ARNOLD, who worked on a coal boat as a cabin boy, ISABEL GUNN, who delivered fur to trading outposts on a canoe, and ANNE JANE THORNTON, who sailed to Maine on an abortive pilgrimage to find the man she had fallen in love with. When she discovered he had already married someone else, she worked her passage back to England, despite being unmasked as a woman, and was described by the Captain as having performed "[the duties of a seaman] to admiration. She would run up the top gallant-sail in any sort of weather and we had a severe passage. Poor girl, she had a hard time of it, she suffered greatly from the wet but she bore it all excellently and was a capital seaman."

MOLL CUTPURSE – born Mary Frith – spent most of her career as a pickpocket, fencer and forger dressed as a man, and apparently prided herself on being the first woman to smoke tobacco. She is thought by some to have been Britain's first highwayman, robbing travellers on Hounslow Heath.

DOROTHY LAWRENCE was a reporter who, with the help of two soldiers she befriended, posed as a man so she could become a soldier, during the First World War, saying "I'll see what an ordinary English girl, without credentials or money, can accomplish". She worked laying mines not far behind the front line for 10 days, before admitting her true identity to the commanding sergeant and being placed under military arrest. She was not allowed to write about her experiences, as had been her original intention, and she was later institutionalised as insane (after she claimed to have been raped) and died in an asylum.

MARY EDWARDS WALKER was a doctor in the American Civil War, and as well as being the only woman to receive the Congressional Medal of Honour for her services therein, was a major proponent of women's rights and regarding dress. Noted during her lifetime for her eccentric dress, she married wearing trousers and a man's coat (and kept her own name, unusually for the period) and appeared at public occasions in full men's evening dress, including a top hat, with her hair in feminine curls. She was elected President of the National Association for Dress Reform in 1866, and was also one of America's first female journalists.

JAN MORRIS fathered 5 children as a man before becoming one of the first transsexuals to tell their story publicly, after her gender reassignment surgery in 1972. She continues to be a popular and successful journalist and travel writer.

Six foot four drag queen RU PAUL became the first face of MAC in 1995, and since then has helped raise over $20 million for an AIDS fund run by the cosmetics company.

"I do not impersonate females. How many women do you know who wear seven-inch heels, four-foot wigs, and skintight dresses?"

~

Drag Queens Extraordinaire

Ru Paul
The Lady Chablis
Christine Mancini
Danny La Rue
Lypsinka
Dreuxilla Divine
Dame Edna Everage
Lily Savage
Monet Dupree
Hedda Lettuce

~

War and Peace

MO MOWLAM – To Gerry Adams, before the Good Friday Peace Agreement "Bloody well get on and do it, otherwise I'll head-butt you!"

One of the most popular politicians of recent times, Mo Mowlam helped restore an IRA ceasefire and negotiated the Good Friday Peace Agreement in 1998 as Secretary of State for Northern Ireland – a post that has never before or since been held by a woman. She also visited convicted Loyalist prisoners incarcerated in the infamous Maze prison, in an attempt to get them to support the peace process.

She continued working through her diagnosis of and treatment for a brain tumour, and when described as looking like a Geordie truck driver by journalist Lynda Lee Potter, said that she "quite liked Geordie truck drivers". She died in 2005.

Honoured by *Time* magazine as one of the 100 most important people of the 20th century, **ROSA PARKS** was at the centre of the civil rights movement in America because of her now famous refusal to give up her bus seat to a white man in Montgomery City. Her action, or rather, inaction, sparked a mass boycott of the city's buses by the black community that was to change history. Rosa helped to distribute shoes to people wearing their shoes out walking to work rather than take the bus. Along with many others, she and her husband lost their jobs. The boycott lasted over a year, ending with the ruling that segregation was unconstitutional, and this ruling sparked similar boycotts across the country. Segregation eventually collapsed, the process culminating in the passing of the Civil Rights Act in 1964.

"How she sat there, the time right inside a place so wrong it was ready"
(from 'Rosa' in 'On the Bus with Rosa Parks' by Rita Dove)

FLORA SANDES started her military career in a nursing unit with the St John's Ambulance Brigade, with whom she travelled to Serbia in 1914, but she went on to become an active soldier, fighting for seven years on the front line, and became a Captain in 1926. She was awarded Serbia's highest decoration, the King George Star.

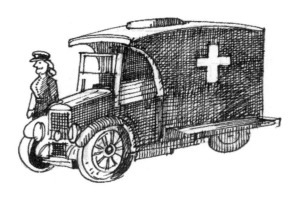

BERTHA VON SUTTNER – inspirer of the Nobel Peace Prize itself because of her friendship with Alfred Nobel, Baroness von Suttner was awarded the Prize in 1905. Her involvement with the Peace League inspired her to write an extremely influential novel about the effects of war, called *Lay Down Your Arms*, and she continued to work in the peace movement from this point on. She established the Austrian Peace Society, and co-established a peace journal. In the lead up to World War I she spoke all over Europe for the cause of peace, despite her worsening health, and she died shortly after the outbreak of the war she had battled against for so long.

The next woman to be awarded the prize was JANE ADDAMS, an American social worker and internationalist, in 1931. Daughter of a banker and senator, her travels in Europe opened her eyes to the extent of urban poverty, and she bought Hull House in Chicago in 1889 and began to provide aid and support for immigrants. Her work in Chicago led to her being called 'the greatest woman who ever lived' by the City Council. Her papers on urban social issues had national influence, and she was vocal both in her support of the suffrage movement, and her opposition of America's involvement in the First World War. This opinion made her unpopular; she was expelled from the organisation, Daughters of the American Revolution and called by them 'the most dangerous woman in America today'. And she wasn't afraid to get her hands dirty – quite literally, when she accepted the post of garbage inspector of the 19th ward of Chicago. She became the first woman to be awarded an honorary degree by Yale University, in 1910.

EMILY GREENE BALCH was a professor and lecturer in economics and sociology, and life-long pacifist, who was awarded the Prize in 1946.

BETTY WILLIAMS was a housewife and one of the first people who came across the tragic scene of three children who had been killed by the getaway car used by an IRA gunman. Appalled by what she had witnessed, she assembled hundreds of local people, including the aunt of the dead children, MAIREAD CORRIGAN, and the two women led huge marches through the streets of Belfast, with Protestants and Catholics walking side by side in protest at the violence. They were jointly awarded the Peace Prize in 1976.

MOTHER TERESA's work in the slums of Calcutta made her probably the most famous nun in the world. She was awarded the Peace Prize in 1979, and was beatified by Pope John Paul II in 2003, earning her the right to be known as Blessed Teresa.

ALVA MYRDAL was awarded the Peace Prize in 1982, partially for her work establishing Sweden's welfare state, as Swedish Ambassador to India, Ceylon and Burma, and on the United Nations Disarmament Committee.

AUNG SAN SUU KYI was still under military detention in Burma when she was awarded the Peace prize in 1991, and her award had to be accepted on her behalf by her husband

and two sons. A devout Buddhist, her founding of the National League for Democracy and non-violent protests against the harsh and oppressive regime led to her detention without trial for 'endangering the state', and 6 years spent under house arrest, in the 1990s, and she was re-arrested in 2003, where she remains to this day. Her husband, a British citizen, was refused entry to Burma while suffering from prostate cancer, and he died without being reunited with his wife, as she knew she would never be allowed to return to the country once she had left.

"It is not power that corrupts but fear. Fear of losing power corrupts those who wield it and fear of the scourge of power corrupts those who are subject to it."

RIGOBERTA MENCHU TUM was a slightly controversial recipient of the Peace Prize, in 1992, because of accusations that she had taken part in violent protests in Guatemala, as part of her work as an activist fighting for the rights of the indigenous population. However these claims have never been substantiated.

JODY WILLIAMS is the founding coordinator of the International Campaign to Ban Landmines, is the chief strategist for the campaign, and was awarded the Peace Prize in 1997.

THE GREENHAM COMMON WOMEN'S PEACE CAMP spent 19 years camping around RAF Greenham Common airbase, campaigning against the decision to site Cruise nuclear missiles there. Living in primitive conditions and frequently attacked and evicted, the women's non-violent and tenacious protest was instrumental in the missiles removal from

Greenham Common. Hundreds of women participated in the protest over the years, with 30,000 women joining hands to 'embrace the base' at one point.

PEACE PILGRIM (Mildred Norma Ryder) walked over 25,000 miles between 1953 and 1981 in a campaign for peace and disarmament. She travelled penniless, carrying no belongings other than a toothbrush, comb and pen, relying on the kindness of strangers for food and shelter.

She experienced a vision of herself walking cross-country for peace, and, on January first 1953, she set off from Pasadena to New York, wearing a dark tunic embroidered with her new adopted name of Peace Pilgrim. Her message was simple: This is the way of peace: Overcome evil with good, falsehood with truth, and hatred with love.

During her extraordinary journey she crossed the United States seven times, visiting every state capital and also crossing Canada and Mexico.

Pacifist, poet and memoirist VERA BRITTAIN was the author of the best-selling *Testament of Youth* which documents her experiences as a volunteer nurse in Europe, and is often referred to as a 'memorial for a lost generation'. She worked as a fire warden during World War I, and raised money for the food relief campaign run by the Peace Pledge union.

To My Brother (In Memory of July first, 1916)

Your battle-wounds are scars upon my heart,
Received when in that grand and tragic 'show'
You played your part,
Two years ago,

And silver in the summer morning sun
I see the symbol of your courage glow –
That cross you won
Two years ago.

Though now again you watch the shrapnel fly,
And hear the guns that daily louder grow,
As in July,
Two years ago.

May you endure to lead the Last Advance
And with your men pursue the flying foe
As once in France
Two years ago.

HELEN SUZMAN has used her considerable political influence to fight the battle against apartheid in South Africa. She also established a foundation to promote equality and work to address social problems of the country such as unemployment, crime and HIV/AIDS.

LOUISE MICHEL or the *Red Virgin of Montmartre*, as she is sometimes known, was an anarchist who fought in the

French revolution of the 19th century, and in the Paris Commune, which fought for a social revolution. After her arrest for her part in this uprising, she spent over 6 years in exile, before an amnesty allowed her to return to her home country, but she continued to demonstrate and fight the anarchist cause of "bread for all, knowledge for all, work for all, independence and justice for all" until her death in 1905.

BOUDICCA was the wife of the leader of the Iceni, a tribe based in what is now an area between Suffolk and Norfolk. Following his death and the pillaging of his property by

Romans in 60, Boudicca gathered up troops and took the lead role in the battle to reclaim power from Emperor Nero. Although she eventually lost the battle, and committed suicide by drinking poison, her actions apparently encouraged the occupying Romans to treat Britons with a bit more compassion. Now the bronze image of her leading her troops into battle overlooks Victoria Embankment, in London, and she is said to be buried beneath Track 10 at King's Cross Station.

No woman has served as Secretary General of the United Nations.

Women's Women

~

GERMAINE GREER, author of *The Female Eunuch*, is one of the 20th century's most important and influential feminist writers and thinkers, and one of the most controversial figures in the field. The impact of *The Female Eunuch* on society cannot be over-estimated, as Lisa Jardine points out.

"Greer's detractors may pooh-pooh its influence, but the fact is that for women born in the immediate postwar years there was 'before Greer' and 'after Greer'. The book, and Germaine's attention-grabbing brand of stand-up-comic, in-your-face assertiveness, taught us all how to behave badly and take control of our lives. She was Mae West, Dorothy Parker and Gertrude Stein rolled into one, with a touch of the self-parodying Lenny Henrys."

Arrested in New Zealand in 1972 for swearing in her talks, called everything from "the ultimate Trojan horse, gorgeous and witty" to "a clever fool", she continues to polarise opinions and provoke debate. Initially a Shakespearean scholar, she has written passionately on fertility, divorce, aging and sexuality, refusing to be swayed by criticism.

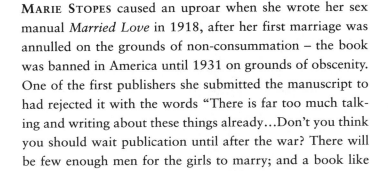

JO BRAND'S HEROINES

I admire any woman who steps outside of the narrow confines of male/societal expectations. I also admire any female comic who is prepared to make herself look appalling for the sake of a laugh. Therefore my heroines are:

Victoria Wood
Dawn French
Linda Smith
Caroline Aherne
Bessie Smith
Sylvia Pankhurst
Janet Street Porter
Germaine Greer
My Mum.

And hundreds of others too numerous to mention.

MARIE STOPES caused an uproar when she wrote her sex manual *Married Love* in 1918, after her first marriage was annulled on the grounds of non-consummation – the book was banned in America until 1931 on grounds of obscenity. One of the first publishers she submitted the manuscript to had rejected it with the words "There is far too much talking and writing about these things already...Don't you think you should wait publication until after the war? There will be few enough men for the girls to marry; and a book like this would frighten off the few." Three years after its publication, Stopes, together with her second husband, opened

Britain's first family planning clinic, in Islington, in the face of strong opposition from both the Catholic Church and the medical establishment.

"A modern and human civilization must control contraception or sink into barbaric cruelty to individuals."
Marie Stopes, 1923.

Marie Stopes's interest in birth control had been sparked by meeting **MARGARET SANGER**, an American birth control campaigner who was herself one of 11 children, and whose work as a nurse in the New York slums had convinced her of the dangers of self-induced abortions, and the problems of raising large families in poor conditions. Opposition to the discussion of such matters at the time was such that discussion of contraception was outlawed as obscene, and her family planning clinic in Brooklyn (the first of its kind in America) was closed, and Sanger arrested, in 1916.

"No woman can call herself free who does not own and control her body. No woman can call herself free until she can choose consciously whether she will or will not be a mother." 1920

DOROTHEA BEALE (founder of St Hilda's College, Oxford and Principal of Cheltenham Ladies' College) and FRANCES BUSS (headmistress for 44 years of the North London Collegiate School) were redoubtable Victorian supporters of women's education – so much so that they inspired the rhyme:

Miss Buss and Miss Beale
Cupid's darts do not feel.
How different from us,
Miss Beale and Miss Buss.

An earlier advocate of the ideas of Miss Beale and Miss Buss was MARY WOLLSTONECRAFT, whose book *Thoughts on the Education of Daughters* was the first of her feminist writings, the most famous of which, *Vindication of the Rights of Women*, argued against the commonly held view that women were inherently inferior to men. She died of fever following the birth of her daughter, Mary, who would grow up to marry Percy Bysshe Shelley, and write *Frankenstein*.

BETTY FRIEDAN *The Feminine Mystique*, published in 1963, created thousands of feminists with its attack on the idea that women's only useful role was that of a housewife, and according to Germaine Greer, Friedan "changed the course of human history almost single-handedly".

An opponent of the 'equation of feminism with lesbianism' early in her career, she later pledged her support for the lesbian rights movement at a conference in 1977 to approve the UN's 'Platform for Women'. Its approval was a defining moment for the American Women's Movement.

CATHERINE GRIFFITHS was a suffragette who was jailed for breaking into the House of Lords, where she had spread nails on Lloyd George's seat 'to make him sit up'.

FERN BRITTON'S HEROINES

The Queen – the greatest exponent of "say nothing.
It will pass".
Diana, Princess of Wales – her passion, frailty and
fortitude.
Camilla, Duchess of Cornwall – weakness and courage.
Fiona Bruce – authority, serenity and humour.
Jane Russell and Lauren Bacall – real women's women.
My mum – just about everything.

THELMA CAZALET-KEIR, a Conservative MP during the Second World War, was responsible for Churchill's only House of Commons war-time defeat, over an Education Bill proposing equal pay for male and female teachers. A member of the renowned Cazalet family, she was told by Lloyd George that she was "one of the two women who never bore me".

BELLA ABZUG was a lawyer who campaigned for welfare reform and against the war, and was the first Jewish woman to be elected to Congress. Famous for the large hats she wore (to distinguish her from secretaries, she claimed) as much as for her political views, she was, nevertheless, a force to be reckoned with who made great strides in the American women's movement and led 1,000 Vietnam veterans in an anti-war demonstration on Capitol Hill.

MARY PHELPS JACOBS, a socialite in New York around the turn of the century, solved the problem of her corset showing through her thin dress, by constructing a support mechanism from some ribbon and handkerchiefs, and the modern bra was born. She patented her 'contraption' in 1914 and later sold it to the Warner Brothers Corset Company for $1,500.

BARBARA CASTLE: "In politics, why throw away your womanly assets on being an honorary man? You should have the strength that women have and to call it a man's strength is an insult."

MP for 34 years, and champion of pensioners' rights, Barbara Castle was also a leading light in the campaign for equal pay for women, the Act proposing which she carried through parliament in 1970, along with the 70 mile an hour speed limit and the introduction of breathalysers.

Victorian feminist JOSEPHINE BUTLER became closely involved with the welfare of prostitutes and the repeal of the Contagious Diseases Act, which allowed women living in military towns to be forcibly examined for VD. She also campaigned against child prostitution, succeeding in raising the age of consent to sexual activity from 13 to 16.

The fight over votes for women was characterised by hunger strikes, women chaining themselves to railings and public protests in the streets. The death of EMILY DAVISON under the King's horse at the Epsom Derby, in 1913 was the culmination of her direct action in support of the movement, which had included hiding in a cupboard in Westminster on the night of the 1911 census in order to legally give her address on the forms as that of the House of Commons. EMMELINE PANKHURST, and her daughters CHRISTABEL and SYLVIA, were some of the highest profile suffragettes, who drew the most attention to the campaign. She was also important in the protests that led to women being allowed to take men's jobs during World War I, which freed more men to be drafted to fight.

~

Deeds Not Words: British Suffragettes

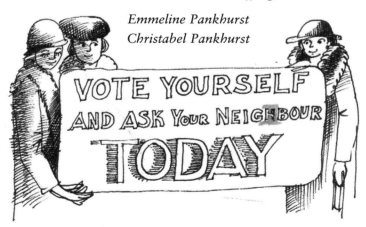

Emmeline Pankhurst
Christabel Pankhurst

Sylvia Pankhurst
Emily Davison
Emily Davies
Rosa May Billingshurst
Annie Kenney

CHRISTINE DE PISAN managed to work as a writer in the male-dominated medieval literary world. She wrote of women's contributions to society, and a long poem on Joan of Arc, and criticised the way women were portrayed in literature, displaying in doing so attitudes centuries ahead of her time.

The Women's Room, the most famous work by novelist MARILYN FRENCH, portrays the lives of housewives and mothers in 1950s American suburbia, and had a huge impact on the way thousands of women lived and thought when it was published in the 1970s.

SIMONE DE BEAUVOIR is seen by some as the founder of contemporary feminism, with her book *The Second Sex*, first published in 1949. In this, she proposes that women are not born as such, but made, and that women are seen as deviant from the norm of masculinity. She was also an important existential philosopher, and had a long relationship, both romantic and intellectual, with fellow philosopher Jean Paul Sartre. On her death in 1986 headlines proclaimed "Women, you owe her everything!".

More about Bold, Bad and Beautiful Women

~

There are literally thousands of biographies of the women mentioned in this book, so this is just a few that I have found particularly useful, and doesn't include any of the ones already mentioned throughout the book.

Hell's Belles: A Tribute to the Spitfires, Bad Seeds and Steel Magnolias of the New and Old South by Seale Ballenger

The Women Who Lived for Danger: The Women Agents of SOE in the Second World War, by Marcus Binney

America's Queen: The Life of Jacqueline Kennedy Onassis, by Sarah H. Bradford

Rosa Parks by Douglas G. Brinkley

America's Women: 400 Years of Dolls, Drudges, Helpmates and Heroines, by Gail Collins

The Six Wives of Henry VIII, by Antonia Fraser

The Diary of Frida Kahlo: An Intimate Self-Portrait by Carlos Fuentes

Annabel: An Unconventional Life, by Annabel Goldsmith

Palgrave Macmillan Dictionary of Women's Biography, by Maggy Hendry and Jenny Uglow

Courtesans, by Katie Hickman

They Went Whistling: Women Wayfarers, Warriors, Runaways and Renegades, by Barbara Holland

Mistresses of Mayhem: The Book of Women Criminals, by Francine Hornberger

The Final Confession of Mabel Stark, by Robert Hough

Love, Janis by Laura Joplin

Marilyn Monroe, by Barbara Leaming

The Mitford Girls, by Mary S. Lovell

Judi Dench: With a Crack in Her Voice, by John Miller

Hons and Rebels by Jessica Mitford

Madame de Pompadour, by Nancy Mitford

Words of Love: Passionate Women from Heloise to Sylvia Plath by Pamela Norris

Sharon Osbourne Extreme: My Autobiography by Sharon Osbourne

The Vogue Book of Blondes, by Kathy Phillips

Being Jordan and *A Whole New World*, by Katie Price

Chin Up, Girls! A Book of Women's Obituaries from The Daily Telegraph, edited by Georgia Powell and Katharine Ramsay

The Courtesans, by Joanna Richardson

Open Secret: The Autobiography of the Former Director-General of MI5, by Stella Rimington

Unsuitable for Ladies: An Anthology of Women Travellers, by Jane Robinson

The Honest Courtesan, by Margaret F. Rosenthal

Madonna: An Intimate Biography, by J. Randy Taraborelli

The Strange History of Bonnie and Clyde, by John E. Treherne

Powder Puff Derby: Petticoat Pilots and Flying Flappers, by Mike Walker

Audrey Hepburn: Fair Lady of the Screen, by Ian Woodward

Moments of Being: Autobiographical Writings, by Virginia Woolf

Acknowledgements

Huge thanks to all the people who have helped me in the writing of this book by suggesting names, sending me biographical information, lending and giving me books, helped me thrash out the definition of exactly what a heroine is, contributing lists, and in all sorts of other ways. Particular thanks to my family for their encouragement and support, and to my husband Jack, for patiently enduring a decline in attention from his wife and a rise in the number of books about 'women and stuff' all over the house and continuing to listen and talk to me about it all. Thank you.

Lynn Abrams, Louise Ansdell, Polly Atkin, Catherine Baigent, Lucy Baker, Suzy Baker, Immodesty Blaize, Cherie Booth, Jo Brand, Christina Bretten, James Bretten, Emma Bridgewater, Fern Britton, Olivia Browne, Dee Cahill, Michael Cannons, Anna Cheetham, Tim Coates, Jilly Cooper, Alana Cox, Anthony Cox, Rhys Davies, Josceline Dimbleby, Walter Essex, Bernard Fancher, Julie Ferris, Julian Flanagan, Clara Freeman, Hadley Freeman, Sarah Frost Mellor, Adèle Geras, Vivien Green, Geordie Greig, Annabel

Goldsmith, Lisa Guidarini, Lulu Guinness, Sally Gunnell, Sarah Harman, Lynne Hatwell, Susan Hill, Gur Hirshberg, Jacob Hurst, P. D. James, Ros Jay, Roz Jenkins, Charlie Lee Potter, Kathy Lette, Tijen Levent, Ashleigh Lezard, James Long, Candida Lycett Green, Sue MacGregor, Kirstie MacLaren, Will MacLaren, Sophie Mackenzie, David Mackinder, Evie Martin, Julie Martin, Will Martin, Carla McKay, Caroline Michel, Caroline Mileham, Bel Mooney, Elizabeth Neville, Scott Pack, Tara Palmer-Tomkinson, Sara Parker Bowles, Katie Pertwee, Zoe Peto, Hazel Phillips, Claudia Roden, Alex Ruston, Jack Ruston, Joe Ruston, Judy Ruston, Liz Scarboro, Caroline Scott, Elaine Simpson-Long, Alexandra Simonon, Lucy Singh, Anna Slade, Helen Slavin, Brian Smith, Suzy Smith, Alan Sommerstein, Lynda Swaffield, Vara Szajkowski, Helen Taylor, Sophy Topley, Joanna Trollope, Penny Vincenzi, Jasmine Ward, Anita Warren, Clemency Wells, Stanley Wells, Mike Wharton

Index

~

Bionic Woman, The 147
Black Beauty 188, 189
Blackwell, Elizabeth 56-7
Blaise, Modesty 150
Blaize, Immodesty 150
Blanchard, Madame Sophie 123
Blanchett, Cate 86
Blandings, the Empress of 189
Blyton, Enid 102
Boleyn, Anne 27, 112
Bombalurina 189
Bonny, Anne 136
Booth, Cherie (Cherie Blair) 54-55, 56
Borgia, Lucrezia 138
Boudicca (Boadicea) 27, 202-03
Bouvier, Pam 32
Bovary, Madame 105, 179
Bracken, Peg 49-50
Bradley, Eliza 163
Bradshaw, Carrie 85
Brand, Jo 205
Bridgewater, Emma 184-5
Brinkley, Christie 80
Brittain, Vera 200-01
Britton, Fern 208
Brooks, Geraldine 103
Brooks, Louise 77
Bruce, Fiona 208
Brunhilde 24
Buck, Pearl S. 61, 101
Buck, Linda B. 169
Buckingham, Christine 133
Bullwinkel, Vivian 70
Bündchen, Gisele 86
Bunton, Emma 130
Burton, Lady Isabel 174
Buss, Frances 207
Butler, Josephine 209-10
Butterfly, Madame 131, 180
Buxton, Dorothy 111

C, Mel (Melanie Chisholm) 130
Calil, Carmen 109
Callas, Maria 107, 130
Campbell, Naomi 79
Caria, Artemisia 175
Carleton, Mary 139-40

Carmen 131
Carson, Rachel 168
Carter, June 184-85
Cartland, Dame Barbara 175-76
Casati, The Marchesa Luisa 64-66
Case, Tiffany 32
Cassandra 189
Cassatt, Mary 183
Castle, Barbara 209
Catarina 189
Catherine the Great 24-26
Catwoman 147
Cavell, Edith 90
Cazalet-Keir, Thelma 208
Chablis, The Lady 194
Chanel, Coco 66, 77, 145
Charlotte 189
Chatterley, Lady 179
Child, Julia 48, 49
Church, Ellen 123
Ciccone, Madonna 127, 132, 150, 155
Cinderella 18
Clarissa 105
Cleopatra 11, 82-83, 94, 173
Cleves, Anne of 112-13
Clinton, Hillary Rodham 60
Clitheroe, Saint Margaret 99
Clock, Arietty 69
Cochran, Jacqueline 120
Cochrane, Josephine 46
Cole, Natalie 133
Coleman, Bessie 122
Colette 64, 107
Connolly, Jennifer 86
Constantine, Susannah 144
Coppola, Sofia 85
Cori, Gerty 169
Cornioley, Pearl 124
Cornwall, Camilla, Duchess of 208
Corrigan, Mairead 198
Creighton-Ward, Lady Penelope 34
Croft, Lara 69
Curie, Marie 61-62, 141